D1246133

Exploring Feelings for Young Children with High-Functioning Autism or Asperger's Disorder

by the same author

The Complete Guide to Asperger's Syndrome
Tony Attwood
ISBN 978 1 84310 495 7 (hardback)
ISBN 978 1 84310 669 2 (paperback)
eISBN 978 1 84642 559 2

Asperger's Syndrome
A Guide for Parents and Professionals
Tony Attwood
Foreword by Lorna Wing
ISBN 978 1 85302 577 8
eISBN 978 1 84642 697 1

of related interest

The Red Beast
Controlling Anger in Children with Asperger's Syndrome
K.I. Al-Ghani
Illustrated by Haitham Al-Ghani
ISBN 978 1 84310 943 3
eISBN 978 1 84642 848 7

Asperkids
An Insider's Guide to Loving, Understanding and Teaching
Children with Asperger Syndrome
Jennifer Cook O'Toole
Foreword by Liane Holliday Willey
ISBN 978 1 84905 902 2
eISBN 978 0 85700 647 9

Teaching Theory of Mind
A Curriculum for Children with High Functioning Autism,
Asperger's Syndrome, and Related Social Challenges
Kirstina Ordetx
Foreword by Susan J. Moreno
ISBN 978 1 84905 897 1

Managing Meltdowns
Using the S.C.A.R.E.D. Calming Technique with Children and
Adults with Autism
Deborah Lipsky and Will Richards
ISBN 978 1 84310 908 2
eISBN 978 1 84642 917 0

Exploring Feelings for Young Children with High-Functioning Autism or Asperger's Disorder

The STAMP Treatment Manual

Angela Scarpa, Anthony Wells and Tony Attwood

Jessica Kingsley *Publishers*
London and Philadelphia

First published in 2013
by Jessica Kingsley Publishers
73 Collier Street
London N1 9BE, UK
and
400 Market Street, Suite 400
Philadelphia, PA 19106, USA

www.jkp.com

Copyright © Angela Scarpa, Anthony Wells and Tony Attwood 2013
Illustrations copyright © Paileen Currie 2013

Front cover image source: Veer. The cover image is for illustrative purposes only, and any person featuring is
a model.

All rights reserved. No part of this publication may be reproduced in any material form (including
photocopying of any pages other than those marked with a ✓, or storing it in any medium by electronic
means and whether or not transiently or incidentally to some other use of this publication) without the
written permission of the copyright owner except in accordance with the provisions of the Copyright,
Designs and Patents Act 1988 or under the terms of a licence issued by the Copyright Licensing Agency
Ltd, Saffron House, 6–10 Kirby Street, London EC1N 8TS. Applications for the copyright owner's written
permission to reproduce any part of this publication should be addressed to the publisher.

Warning: The doing of an unauthorized act in relation to a copyright work may result in both a civil claim
for damages and criminal prosecution.

All pages marked ✓ may be photocopied for personal use with this program, but may not be reproduced for
any other purposes without the permission of the publisher.

Library of Congress Cataloging in Publication Data
Scarpa, Angela, author.
  Exploring feelings for young children with high-functioning autism or Asperger's disorder : the STAMP
treatment manual / Angela Scarpa, Anthony Wells, and Tony Attwood
     pages cm
  ISBN 978-1-84905-920-6 (alk. paper) -- ISBN 978-0-85700-681-3 1. Asperger's syndrome in
children--
Treatment. 2. Autistic children--Rehabilitation. 3. Cognitive therapy for children. I. Wells, Anthony,
author. II. Attwood, Tony, author. III. Title.

  RJ506.A4S33 2013
  618.92'858832--dc23

                          2012024377

British Library Cataloguing in Publication Data
A CIP catalogue record for this book is available from the British Library

ISBN 978 1 84905 920 6
eISBN 978 0 85700 681 3

Printed and bound in Great Britain by Bell and Bain Ltd, Glasgow

To Hugh, who inspired this program,
and to all the families with whom we
have had the privilege to work.
You have taught us so much.

MAY 3 0 2017

Acknowledgments

The authors would like to extend our appreciation to all the children and families who participated in STAMP and shaped the development of this manual. We would also like to give a special thanks to Nuri Reyes who helped to pilot test the program and to all our STAMP therapists and assistants over the years. In particular, Jill Lorenzi, Tyler Hassenfeldt, Katrina Ostmeyer, Jiwon Choi, Katie Leslie, and Caitlin Kirkwood were instrumental in the final revisions of the STAMP manual.

CONTENTS

LIST OF RESOURCES

PART 1

Introduction

1

OVERVIEW

This manual outlines the Stress and Anger Management Program (STAMP), which is a structured treatment that provides children with high-functioning autism (HFA) or Asperger's disorder with a set of strategies for decreasing negative feelings and increasing positive feelings in daily life. The program is considered an extension of Dr. Tony Attwood's cognitive-behavioral program for children with HFA and Asperger's disorder who may suffer from mood difficulties, particularly anger and anxiety (Sofronoff, Attwood, & Hinton, 2005; Sofronoff, Attwood, Hinton, & Levin, 2007). Dr. Attwood's treatment was developed for middle childhood (ages 9–13 years old), yet STAMP addresses the needs of early childhood (ages 5–7 years old) using methods that are more developmentally appropriate for younger children. Even more important than the age of the child is the consideration of the child's developmental level, which should be in the range of preschool to first grade. Treatment components of the nine-session program include affective education, cognitive restructuring, and the emotional toolbox (i.e., emotion regulation skills). A parental component is also added to encourage practice at home and therefore promote generalization outside of the therapy setting.

2

BACKGROUND
WANDERING IN THE SOCIAL–EMOTIONAL TERRAIN

Autism was first identified by Kanner (1943) and originally thought to be a relatively rare disorder that affected approximately 3 in 10,000 children. Currently, autism is thought to be the fastest growing neurodevelopmental disability in the United States. A recent survey found that an average of 1 in 88 children is affected with an autism spectrum disorder (ASD) in the United States (Centers for Disease Control and Prevention, 2012). According to current diagnostic criteria (American Psychiatric Association (APA), 1994, 2000), the diagnosis of autism requires impairments in three core areas: social functioning, communication, and repetitive behaviors, interests, or activities—with onset prior to age 3.

At the same time as Kanner's initial work, Asperger (1944) described a group of children with similar characteristics to autism, but who had no language or cognitive delay. This cluster of symptoms is currently referred to as Asperger's disorder and was formally published in the Diagnostic and Statistical Manual of Mental Disorders (4th edition) (DSM-IV) in 1994. In contrast to autism, the Asperger's disorder diagnosis does not require clinically significant delay in language development, self-help skills, adaptive behavior, and curiosity about the environment. There is some dispute regarding the practical differences between Asperger's disorder and HFA. The language delay of autism is the most noticeable difference, yet beyond early childhood, the two diagnoses appear to involve the same fundamental symptomatology (Ozonoff, South, & Miller, 2000), and it is being recommended that the next edition of the DSM collapse these disorders under the umbrella of autism spectrum disorder (ASD).

Youth with ASD demonstrate emotional and behavioral disturbances across the lifespan. For example, children with HFA and Asperger's disorder both present with clinically significant disruptive behaviors, anxiety, and depression (Tonge, Brereton, Gray, & Einfeld, 1999; Kim, Szatmari, Bryson, Streiner, & Wilson, 2000; Gillott, Furniss, & Walter, 2001). Furthermore, they may have difficulty understanding their own inner emotional states and the emotional states of others, which is often referred to as "theory of mind" (Baron-Cohen, Leslie, & Firth, 1985). In addition, these children may not be able to identify or describe feeling states and may not understand their own bodily sensations of emotional arousal (Hill, Berthoz, & Frith, 2004). One reason for the difficulty that children with ASD may have in understanding and managing their emotions involves delays in executive functioning. Executive functioning includes planning, organizing, inhibiting behavior, and regulating arousal. Consequently, children with ASD may appear as difficult to manage, but their difficulties stem from problems with behavior and regulation that are part of executive dysfunction (Klin, McPartland, & Volkmar, 2005).

Therefore, delays in executive functioning can lead to problems regulating emotions. Emotion regulation is defined as the ability to change an ongoing emotion as needed in order to achieve some goal. Developmentally, emotion regulation begins with the infant's ability to self-soothe when physiologically aroused, and is often dependent on the help of caregivers. Such regulation is believed to become more self-guided as the child matures, and these abilities are typically in place by 36 months of age (Kopp, 1982). In addition to executive dysfunction, children with ASD often have additional barriers that interfere with emotion regulation as they grow, including sensory issues, poor facial processing and social orienting in infancy, and difficulties with communication. These challenges can offset early emotion regulation by increasing arousal and frustration and interfering with the ability to use caregivers or others as soothing social agents. Poor emotion management, in turn, can further disrupt learning and social interactions.

3

TREATMENT
DEVELOPMENT
MARCH TOWARD COMPETENCY

For these reasons, it is crucial that we find ways to help children with ASD learn to manage their stress and anger as early as possible. Unfortunately, very few treatments have been developed specifically addressing emotional difficulties in children with ASD. Dr. Tony Attwood and his colleagues have had promising results, however. Their program, called Exploring Feelings, consists of cognitive-behavioral treatments for children with HFA and Asperger's disorder in the middle childhood age range. To date, they have conducted two randomized, controlled trials of the Exploring Feelings cognitive-behavioral program.

One study examined the efficacy of the program for improving anger management (Sofronoff et al., 2007). Forty-five children aged 9–13 with diagnosed Asperger's disorder participated in the study. To be eligible for the study, children had to display the presence of anger. The children were randomly assigned to an intervention group or to a wait-list control group (whose treatment was delayed so they could be compared with those receiving the intervention earlier). The intervention was conducted over six two-hour weekly sessions designed to be highly structured, informative and entertaining. The children were taught anger-management strategies such as relaxation, anger recognition, emotional release and social contact. The children developed individualized plans based on the strategies learned. Meanwhile, the parents engaged in a parent group, where a therapist discussed the principles of the sessions with them. Parents indicated reduced anger episodes and improvement in the areas of frustration, peer relationships and authority relationships. Parents and children also reported increased confidence with managing the child's anger. In a teacher survey, 88 per cent reported a positive change in the children. Of those who noticed a change, 19 per cent reported the child would ask to withdraw from class when angry, and 56 per cent reported that the child would discuss their anger and reduce outbursts.

The other study examined the efficacy of the program for improving anxiety management (Sofronoff *et al.*, 2005). This study also examined whether intensive parental involvement would increase a child's ability to manage anxiety outside of the clinic. Seventy-one children aged 10–12 with diagnosed Asperger's disorder participated in the study. The children had to display anxiety to be eligible for the study. The children were randomly assigned to one of three groups: an intervention group where the child was treated in a group without parents, an intervention group with parental involvement, or a wait-list control group. The intervention was conducted over six two-hour weekly sessions using the same components described above, but specifically targeted anxiety. The reality and probability of their fears were also discussed in one of the sessions. Parents reported overall improvement in their child's anxiety (including obsessive compulsive, generalized anxiety, and social fear tendencies), with greater improvements in the format that added parental involvement. Children in both intervention groups also showed an increase in the strategies they could name to manage anxiety, again with greater increases in the group with parental involvement.

Taken together, these two studies provide support for the use of cognitive-behavioral therapy to treat anger and anxiety in children with HFA/Asperger's disorder. We believe it is critical to now extend the treatment to younger children, since early intervention is optimal and recommended for children with ASD.

4

STAMP

The program described in this manual extends this cognitive-behavioral approach to 5–7-year-old children with HFA or Asperger's disorder. The children are most likely to be in preschool to first grade, so the program uses games and activities that are often seen in these early school years as a means for teaching various skills and concepts. The primary strategies used in this program include: affective education, skill-building (by introducing the emotional toolbox), and cognitive restructuring. Children meet once weekly as a group for one hour per session over nine weeks. Parents meet simultaneously with another therapist who reviews the skills with parents, troubleshoots, and describes practice assignments that the parent and child should do together for the following week.

STAMP Components

Affective Education

Affective education is a term used to mean that we are teaching children about feelings. Specifically, we teach the children the range of both positive and negative emotions and the vocabulary words to be able to express their emotions accurately. The children are also taught the bodily sensations, thoughts, and behaviors that occur when we are upset and that can often serve as early warning signs or clues of emotional escalation.

Skill-Building (The Emotional Toolbox)

The emotional toolbox, a concept developed by Dr. Attwood, is used as part of teaching children ways to handle their anger and anxiety. It is a metaphor of a toolbox with different types of "tools" to help "repair" the problems related to feeling anxiety, anger, or sadness. The tools consist of different strategies that help to release (i.e., physical tools like exercise) or to soothe (i.e., relaxation tools like deep breathing) emotional arousal. Other tools include social, cognitive, and special interest tools to improve help-seeking behaviors, thoughts, and pleasurable activities, respectively.

Cognitive Restructuring

The primary goal of cognitive restructuring is to help the children learn that their thoughts can affect how they feel and act; therefore, they can sometimes change their thoughts to feel better. In cognitive restructuring, the children learn to identify thoughts that may increase their anxiety/anger (e.g., "They will laugh at me") and then replace those thoughts with antidotes (e.g., "I can stay calm"). This is used to challenge distorted thoughts or misinterpretations that may arise out of delayed theory of mind abilities, literal or concrete thinking, or poor pragmatics (both understanding the meaning of a situation as well as seeking clarification of others' comments). The children are also taught that they can use pleasant thoughts to counteract the effects of unpleasant thoughts.

5

SESSION OVERVIEWS

Session 1: Exploring Positive Feelings (Happiness)

The primary goal for the first few sessions is to introduce different feelings. We start with positive feelings in order to develop rapport with the children and begin with a positive tone. The children are more comfortable and find it easier to learn the concepts when we relate it first to happy feelings. Therefore, in the first session we focus on feeling happy and the different degrees of happiness that someone might experience. The Singing and Story Time Activities are used to prime the children for thinking about happy feelings. The Ruler Game is designed to explore degrees of happiness, because children with ASD may have difficulty identifying feelings that are not very strong or that might be early clues that something is bothering them. As part of the game, for example, the child may experience having his favorite cereal at breakfast as satisfying, and place that feeling in the middle of the ruler. Getting presents at his birthday party, however, might be experienced as "exciting," and placed very high on the ruler. We also introduce the purpose and goals of the program. The primary goal of STAMP is to learn how to understand and manage feelings, especially anger and anxiety. The four main reasons we would want to do this are so that we feel better, think better, stay out of trouble, and make friends. Therapists are encouraged to remind the children and parents of the main goal and these reasons regularly throughout the program.

In Session 1, children may not understand where to place their feelings on the ruler and may consistently place all their feelings on either the low end or the high end of the continuum. This is not uncommon, since they often recognize the extremes, but not the middle levels of emotions. Therapists can teach them by comparing the number ratings for each feeling and comparing situations to each other (e.g., "How did you feel when you went to Disneyworld?" versus "How did you feel when you sat down to watch TV?").

Session 2: Exploring Positive Feelings (Relaxation) and Anger/Anxiety—Emotional Toolbox Introduction

Session 2 continues with exploring positive feelings and focuses on the feeling of being relaxed, also introducing the feelings of anger and anxiety and discussing how those feelings compare with feeling relaxed. Because children with ASD may not fully understand how emotions affect us, this session has a strong focus on how we feel inside our bodies and how we act when we are relaxed versus when we are angry or anxious. We start with defining and describing the feelings of anger and anxiety, and perform several activities. The Singing and Story Activities are used to help the children start thinking about relaxation. The Body Trace Activity is used to describe bodily sensations associated with relaxation (such as a slow-beating heart, slow breathing, loose muscles), and then we will contrast relaxed feelings with angry and anxious feelings (such as a fast heart, heavy breathing, tense muscles). Finally, the "emotional toolbox" is introduced to provide the children with a set of tools they can use to "fix" their feelings of anger and anxiety. The toolbox includes physical tools, relaxation tools, social tools, thinking tools, and special interest tools. These tools provide strategies based on relaxation, energy release, social contact, and changing thoughts. The emotional toolbox forms the crux of STAMP and is reviewed in detail in each of the remaining sessions.

In Session 2, it is very important to provide simple definitions of anger and anxiety because young children may not understand what those words mean. Anger is described as when children sometimes feel mad, annoyed, frustrated, or even furious. Anxiety is described as when children feel scared, worried, or nervous about something that they think might happen. Children also need help recognizing the physical signs of anxiety or anger in their bodies, and it is helpful to have an assistant point to places on the body trace where bodily arousal might be felt.

Session 3: Exploring Anxiety and Anger, and Physical and Relaxation Tools

This session will continue to focus on anger, anxiety, and the emotional toolbox— options for cooling down when we get angry or anxious. The Ruler Game, introduced in Session 1, is used to explore degrees of anger/anxiety. The main point to get across is that it is often more successful to use the tools at lower levels of anger/anxiety, before the feeling gets too strong. This session focuses specifically on physical and relaxation tools. Physical tools are described as tools that raise our heart rates and release energy. Relaxation tools lower our heart rates and energy and make us feel calm. The children participate in activities where they move to accelerate their breathing and heart rate, and then they use a relaxation tool to slow their breathing and heart rate. A monitor can be used so the children can actually see their heart rates going up and down to illustrate the powerful effect of physical and relaxation tools on their bodies. If a monitor is not available, simply having the children feel their chest moving up and down is also a good method to demonstrate the effect. Sometimes, children have a difficult time becoming still after they have activated themselves with a physical tool—therapists can help by having the child sit on a chair or the floor, using a calm voice to direct the child, and breathing slowly along with the child. The child is often awed by seeing their breathing and heart rate slow down at this point.

Session 4: Social Tools

Session 4 moves to exploring social tools to cool down. The focus is on using social contact as a method for managing feelings. In this session, we discuss how the child can help others when others feel anxious or angry. We also discuss how others can help the child when he or she feels anxious or angry. The children are taught a specific script to ask for help when they have a problem or are feeling angry or anxious (i.e., "I have a problem. Can you help me?"). This is particularly important in children with ASD because their social disability can interfere with the view of others as social agents who can help them feel better. In other words, these children may not find it natural to seek others for comfort or help. In addition, sensory issues can actually make physical affection uncomfortable for the child with ASD, leading to avoidance of others who might give them a hug or caress (or other sign of physical affection) in an attempt to comfort the child. Parents are therefore instructed to always ask the child if they can give the child a hug or other form of affection beforehand, and respecting if the child says no. As an assignment after this session, parents and children are asked to interview each other about ways they can help each other to calm down when they are upset. This assignment allows parents to understand specific things that they can do to help their child but, just as importantly, it allows the child to see that he/she can also be a helper. Sometimes, children with ASD do not view themselves as being able to help other people—this knowledge can be a powerful boost to their self-concept.

Session 5: Thinking Tools

Session 5 focuses on how the child can use his or her thoughts as tools to feel better when upset. This can be a difficult concept for some children with ASD to grasp because thoughts are very abstract, whereas children with ASD are often literal thinkers. Therefore, it is important to use strategies that make the concept of "thoughts" as concrete as possible. First, we define thoughts as ideas that we have, and they can be things we *say or see* in our own heads. Second, we use comic strips with thought bubbles to illustrate how someone may be having a thought that others do not hear or know about. We help the child to identify at least one thought that makes them feel good. Finally, we play games that illustrate how thoughts can affect our feelings, and how thoughts can be changed to make us feel better or worse in a situation. Parents are taught how to make a comic strip with thought bubbles, which they will use as an assignment with their child to identify a situation where the child was angry or anxious. They will be asked to draw the event with the people involved and thought bubbles to identify the underlying thought that increased the child's anger/anxiety; then, they will make a new panel with thought bubbles that identify a *modified* thought that could help the child feel better in that situation. The main goal of this session is to help the child connect his/her thoughts with his/her feelings. Many children in this session connect with the idea that they can think of fun things to help themselves feel better. For example, they can think of fun times they had with their grandparents, their favorite pet, a special toy, their last vacation, etc.

Session 6: Special Interest Tools

Many children with ASD have circumscribed interests, and these activities can often be very comforting and enjoyable for the child. As such, they provide a unique tool for helping the child to self-soothe when they are angry or anxious. In this session, the children identify various activities that they enjoy and that could be a special way to make them feel better when they are distressed. For example, some children enjoy reading, blowing bubbles, building models, or listening to music. Some children have very specific interests, such as a particular television show or an event in history. The children make a collage of their interests, and they are encouraged to do or think about these activities when they are beginning to feel angry or anxious. It is important to differentiate between the child using the special interest as a means of escaping from demands or simply for self-stimulation versus using the special interest as a specific means of managing an intense or stressful situation. Parents are encouraged to identify situations where the child typically becomes frustrated or anxious (e.g., before entering a loud and stimulating store) and use the special interest in advance of the situation to help comfort the child, rather than waiting until the child is already upset. They can also suggest that the child uses the tool when they are beginning to feel upset, but for a limited time until the child feels better. This strategy will help prevent the child from getting fixated on the special interest.

Session 7: Appropriate and Inappropriate Tools

This session will focus on understanding the difference between right (appropriate) and wrong (inappropriate) ways to cool down. Since we will discuss all the emotional toolbox of tools as "right ways," this will also serve as an initial review of the program. The children are reminded of the tools we discussed that help us to feel better, but then we also discuss how sometimes we use tools that make us feel worse—like screaming, crying, or hitting. These kinds of tools make us feel worse rather than helping us to stay calm. The children are encouraged to think about the right tools they can use to feel better, think better, stay out of trouble, and make friends. A game is played to help the children identify right and wrong tools, and then they design their own paper toolbox chart to take home. During the week, they will identify on their chart different tools they used that helped them to feel better (right tools) or ended up making them feel worse (wrong tools). As a home assignment, parents are also asked to begin to note the kinds of "right" tools their child typically uses in order to identify patterns of tools that seem to be most helpful for their child. It is important to remind the parents that STAMP provides them and their children with an overview of many tools that people use to manage their feelings, but it is not necessary to use all of those tools. Parents can help their child to identify the tools that seem to be most helpful for them at the present time, and continue to remind them of other tools they may wish to use in the future.

Session 8: Review (Group Story and Create a Commercial)

Session 8 provides a review of the emotional toolbox. The therapists create a story in which the children are used as characters who need to use their tools in order to handle a crisis situation. For example, we have used a story of a fictitious wizard who has stolen all of the children's toys, leaving the children angry and scared. The children in the story take turns coming up with strategies they can use to stay calm so they can solve the problem (e.g., deep breathing, ask for help, do something fun). The story ends when the children use their tools and decide they can have fun with each other without their toys, and the wizard returns all the toys because the children are so smart. Pictures of the children are incorporated into the story to make it likely that they can relate to it. The storybook is given to each child to keep as a reminder of the tools they discussed in STAMP. The remainder of the session is devoted to creating a video of the children each identifying and demonstrating tools they would like to remember. A copy of the video will be made for each child to take home at the next (and final) session. Parents are reminded of the tools discussed in STAMP and asked to review their child's emotional toolbox with their child in the coming week. They are also asked to complete behavior monitoring sheets in order to assess any changes that have taken place in their child's emotional outbursts.

Session 9: Group Reward/Celebration!

This is the final session of STAMP. The session focuses on review, assessments, and celebration for completing the program. The review consists of watching the video that was made in Session 8, which the children take home with them as a reminder of what they learned in the program. Providing each child with a copy of this video as well as the story created in Session 8 serves as a way to help to maintain skills after the nine-week program has ended. Parents and children are encouraged to read the story and watch the video as often as they would like in order to remember the skills they learned. Parents are also encouraged to keep a "success diary" of times they notice that their child has used their emotion toolbox, and to reward their child for these successes. We conduct some assessments during this session, which we can use to examine outcomes for each child. The session ends with a celebration with the parents and children together. The children are enthusiastically congratulated and presented with certificates of completion to celebrate their accomplishment, and families are thanked for their participation.

Parents often express concern in the last few sessions that their child will lose the gains they have begun to see. The therapist can remind the parents that they have learned all the skills to help their child. Moreover, any changes in the child have been due in large part to the participation and coaching of the parent. It is important to remind parents that they have been a huge part in their child's success.

6

RESEARCH EVIDENCE ON THE EFFECTIVENESS OF STAMP

Dr. Angela Scarpa and her research group at the Virginia Tech Autism Clinic in Blacksburg, Virginia have conducted a "proof-of-concept" randomized controlled study to examine the effectiveness of STAMP as it applies to young children with HFA or Asperger's disorder (Scarpa & Reyes, 2011). This study was designed as an initial test to determine if the program overall appears helpful and should be studied further. The purpose of STAMP was to reduce reported and observed levels of anxiety and anger in the children as well as to increase parental confidence in managing child behaviors related to these feelings. Eleven 5–7-year-old children with an ASD diagnosis were recruited to participate in the study and randomly assigned into a treatment or waitlist control group. The waitlist control group waited for the first treatment group to be completed, and then they also received the treatment. In this way, it was possible to compare the treatment group with another group of children who were not yet receiving STAMP.

Prior to beginning STAMP, the presence of problems with anger/anxiety was established using parent and child interview and questionnaires (see Appendices B and C), and ASD diagnosis was confirmed with the Autism Diagnostic Observation Schedule. Children also were required to be verbal and able to follow basic spoken directions. This was necessary in order to select children who could comprehend the stories and instruction provided in STAMP. Measures were taken on two occasions— pre-treatment and immediately post-treatment for both groups—and then again for the waitlist group after receiving treatment. Clinical psychology graduate students and a master's level occupational therapist implemented the program. Children met in groups of two to four for nine weekly one-hour sessions in which they were taught to recognize anxiety and anger and to use strategies to manage these emotions, as described above. Parents were placed together to form a parent group that met weekly with another therapist (i.e., psychologist, graduate student, or occupational therapist) at the same time as the child sessions. Parents reviewed the child sessions via video monitoring and learned the components of each session so they could practice with their child at home and other settings.

Several measures were used to assess whether children's anger or anxiety declined and to assess parental confidence in their ability and their child's ability to manage these emotions. First, parents recorded the frequency of their child's anger/anxiety outbursts displayed in a one-week period (see Parent Measure: Behavior Monitoring Sheet, Appendix B). Second, parents rated their child on their negativity/lability and their ability to regulate emotions using the Emotion Regulation Checklist (Shields & Cicchetti, 1997). Third, children were read two stories that were developed for this study (Child Measure: Ben and the Bullies, and Child Measure: James and His Reading Group, Appendix C) and each child was asked to generate strategies for the main character in the story to cope with his anxiety or anger in the situation described. Finally, parents were asked to rate their level of confidence in themselves to manage their child's emotions and their confidence in their child to manage his/her own emotions (Parent Questions, Appendix B). Parental satisfaction in the program was also surveyed (Parent Measure: Consumer Satisfaction/Evaluation Survey, Appendix B).

From pre- to post-treatment, all children had less parent-reported negativity/lability, better parent-reported emotion regulation, and shorter outbursts, and also generated more coping strategies in response to vignettes. Parents also reported increases in their own confidence and their child's ability to deal with anger and anxiety. In a consumer satisfaction survey, all parents reported being satisfied to extremely satisfied with the STAMP program. These findings were initially reported at the 2009 International Meeting for Autism Research in Chicago, IL and published in Scarpa and Reyes (2011).

Further information can be obtained from Dr. Angela Scarpa at ascarpa@vt.edu.

PART 2

Using the Manual

7

HOW TO USE
THIS MANUAL

This manual is designed so that the therapist can conduct each lesson on a session-by-session basis. A lesson plan is developed for each of the nine STAMP sessions, along with guidelines for timing and supplies.

Schedule

Each session follows the same schedule—Cool Down, Welcome, Singing, Story/Discussion, Activity/Game, Snack/Stickers and Goodbyes. The schedule gives the children a sense of predictability and helps with transitions between activities. It is introduced in Session 1 and posted on the wall each subsequent session.

Home Projects

Every session ends with a review of a homework assignment that the child is to complete with their parent before the next session with the purpose of practicing or reminding the child of the main lesson learned. For example, in Session 1, parents are asked to help their children cut out different expressions of happy feelings from magazines or books. The child and parent are to identify the intensity of the happy feeling, from a "little bit happy" to "very, very happy." This project is given to practice the identification and labeling of varying degrees of happy feelings during affective education. Project assignments are reviewed with parents and children at the beginning of the next session.

Lesson Plans

Each lesson plan is divided into three sections—Time, Supplies, and Schedule/Activity.

- Time: This section tells the therapist approximately how much time to devote to each activity. For example, the Cool Down in Session 1 should take about 10 minutes. Timing is extremely important in this program, as each session is intended to take no longer than one hour. Our pilot work indicated that longer sessions are not tolerated as well in this age group. Moreover, it is important to keep a moderate pace in the sessions so the children will stay engaged and not lose interest.

- Supplies: This section lists the supplies needed for each activity within the schedule. This supply list is meant to help therapists easily prepare for each session. Therapists can quickly go through this last column prior to the session and obtain the necessary items. Some items are listed as optional, in case they are not easily available or made. For example, in Session 2, under the section for Singing, the only required supply is the song written on a poster for children to follow along. However, a therapist may also wish to include a CD of the song played on a CD player, if available.

- Schedule/Activity: This section identifies the schedule category (i.e., Cool Down, Welcome, Singing, Story/Discussion, Activity/Game, Snack/Stickers and Goodbyes) as well as the specific activity performed for each part of the schedule. This section is the "meat" of the manual, providing details on therapist instructions and directions for all of the games or activities. It is important to note that the text with the speech bubble symbol 💬 alongside it represents what the therapist is actually going to say to the children. These words are not necessarily meant to be memorized or repeated word for word by the therapist, but are provided as guidelines. Therapists should review this information carefully prior to each session, so that they have a good idea of what they will say to the children and can speak to the children in a natural style and tone of voice.

Parent Handouts

Each session concludes with corresponding handouts and examples of visual aids that can be used for the session activities. A parent handout is also included, which should be copied and distributed to parents during the parent session. The parent handout outlines the schedule and major activity or lesson for each session, and it ends with a description of the home projects.

8 GENERAL TIPS

Because all of the children involved in the treatment have ASD and difficulties with stress or anger management, they may find it challenging to stay focused and engaged throughout a group session. Below are general suggestions to aid in the process of conducting group sessions and to address specific strengths or weaknesses of children with ASDs.

1. Keep the children involved and active throughout the session.
   - Have the children move the arrow on the schedule.
   - Ask them to write on the whiteboard or erase the board.
   - Ask them questions to keep them engaged.
   - Look at each child directly, give praise, and ask for a high-five.
   - Get them to jump, stretch, or illustrate an answer when appropriate.

2. Give lots of praise.
   - Be specific (e.g., I like how you're sitting and waiting. Good looking at me! Nice smile! I love that answer. Smart suggestion!).
   - High-fives or pat on back.
   - Use an exciting/enthusiastic voice.
   - Smile often.

3. Provide structure.
   - Keep a schedule.
   - Keep the pace up.
   - Have teacher in front and children on chairs facing the teacher.

4. Use a reward system.

   ◦ Reinforce children for following group rules and for practicing their tools.

   ◦ Provide reward for appropriate participation.

   ◦ Be liberal with rewards whenever desired behaviors are seen.

5. Visual aids.

   ◦ Use pictures and illustrations whenever possible (suggestions and printables are provided within the manual).

   ◦ Post visuals on the wall or somewhere easily seen by the group.

   ◦ Use gestures as well as words when describing things (e.g., cup hand around ear when saying "Listen," place hand on chest when describing the heart racing).

9

SUITABILITY FOR THE GROUP

STAMP was designed for children who carry a diagnosis of ASD, including autism, Asperger's disorder, or PDD-NOS (pervasive developmental disorder not otherwise specified); however, it can likely be adapted for any child with anger/anxiety difficulties who meets all other eligibility criteria. The activities in STAMP (e.g., singing, crafts, stories) are best suited for children who have developmental levels similar to those in preschool, kindergarten, or early first grade. The program uses a cognitive-behavioral approach to teach children that thoughts, feelings, and actions are connected and that there are specific tools they can use to help them cope with situations that distress them. STAMP relies heavily on verbal instruction and stories to deliver lessons, although we incorporate many visual supplements and games to support learning. Because of the structure of STAMP, however, some children with certain abilities will benefit more than others from this program. Assessing for the suitability for STAMP for each child is recommended. In order to obtain the most benefits from this program, children should meet the following criteria.

1. Be approximately 5–7 years old, functioning at a preschool, kindergarten or first grade level of comprehension and functional verbal communication. Children who are not functioning at a minimum of 4 years old in verbal ability will have difficulty following the stories and conversation in STAMP. Older children may find the program too easy and become bored. Older children are referred to the original Exploring Feelings program by Dr. Tony Attwood for more developmentally appropriate teaching methods.

2. Be able to follow simple verbal instructions, such as "Stay in your seats," "Use nice hands," "Use calm voices," "Sit in a circle." Children who cannot follow these instructions will have difficulty with the rules of the group and with participating in the activities.

3. Be able to stay in the room. For safety reasons, children need to be able to tolerate staying within the boundaries of the room where they can be supervised adequately. Additionally, if children are very active to the point

where they cannot stay in the area, they will miss the lessons/activities and will disrupt the flow of the group.

4. Be able to tolerate songs, music, and simple crafts. STAMP incorporates a lot of singing, music, and simple craft activities, as might be seen in preschool, kindergarten, or first grade. Crafts can include using glue, tape, and scissors. Therapists can assist with the crafts; however, some children may have sensory responses to glue or other materials and it is important to assess if accommodations can be made to allow the child to participate. Songs and music, however, are involved in every session and they are harder to accommodate if a child has strong reactions to them.

5. Be able to play typical early childhood games, such as Duck, Duck, Goose and Musical Chairs. These games are included to make the sessions developmentally appropriate and fun for young children. Lessons are taught within the context of the games. Children who cannot play the games will have a harder time participating in the sessions.

10

ASSESSMENTS

Therapists may be interested in tracking the progress of individual children within the group. Assessments are included in the manual for such clinical use to help evaluate each child's difficulties as well as their suitability for the group treatment. Other standardized assessments can also be added by therapists. The following assessment measures included in the Appendices may be used.

- Parent Measure: What Makes My Child Angry? and Parent Measure: What Makes My Child Anxious? (Appendix B) and Child Measure: What Makes You Angry? and Child Measure: What Makes You Anxious? (Appendix C) can be used before treatment to assess the child's experiences related to anger or anxiety and determine their suitability for the group. If the child does not have difficulties with anger or anxiety, they may not get the full benefit from this program, although they can still learn the skills. These measures can also be used to create individually relevant scenarios for each child during sessions. For example, a given child may indicate prior to treatment that he or she gets angry when "people say mean things about my family." This information can be used for Session 3 (Part 5).

- Parent Measure: Behavior Monitoring Sheet (Appendix B) can be used before and after treatment to assess changes in behavioral outbursts that parents observe. The social vignettes (Child Measure: Ben and the Bullies and Child Measure: James and His Reading Group, Appendix C) can be used before and after treatment to assess changes in the number and quality of emotion management skills that children report. Our prior research has shown that children who have been through the program are able to generate more strategies about how to deal with anger and anxiety. Children can complete the post-treatment vignettes during the final session (Session 9). The post-treatment Behavior Monitoring Sheet (Resource 20) is distributed in Session 8 so parents can track their child's outbursts for the following week and then return the chart at the last session (Session 9). Our prior research has shown that parents report fewer and shorter outbursts in their children after the STAMP intervention.

- Parent Measure: Consumer Satisfaction/Evaluation Survey (Appendix B) is optional for parent feedback at the end of treatment and is administered during Session 9.

Other standardized measures can be used to aid in determining the child's suitability for STAMP and changes after treatment. Some measures we have used are described here.

- Preschool Anxiety Scale (PAS) (Spence, Rapee, McDonald, & Ingram, 2001): This parent-report scale is based on the Spence Children's Anxiety Scale and was developed to assess the severity of anxiety symptoms in preschool aged children (ages 3–5 years old). Since many children with ASD are emotionally less mature than peers, this scale is thought to be developmentally appropriate. The scale assesses six domains of anxiety including generalized anxiety, panic/agoraphobia, social phobia, separation anxiety, obsessive-compulsive disorder and physical injury fears. It is designed to be relatively easy and quick for parents to complete, normally taking only around ten minutes. Information about the scale can be obtained from www.scaswebsite.com.

- Aberrant Behavior Checklist—Community Form (ABC) (Aman, Singh, Stewart, & Field,1985): The ABC is a symptom checklist for assessing problem behaviors in developmentally challenged individuals within multiple settings, such as the home, school, or workplace. It measures behaviors falling into five subscales: Irritability and Agitation, Lethargy and Social Withdrawal, Stereotypic Behavior, Hyperactivity and Noncompliance, and Inappropriate Speech. It has been used for individuals ranging from 6–54 years old and takes about 10–15 minutes to complete. It can be completed by parents, special educators, psychologists, direct caregivers, nurses, and others with knowledge of the person being assessed. The Irritability and Agitation subscale seems especially relevant for behaviors targeted in STAMP. More information can be obtained from www.stoeltingco.com.

- Social Competence Behavior Evaluation-30 (SCBE-30) (LaFreniere & Dumas, 1996): This scale assesses social abilities in children 30–78 months. It includes three subscales that assess cooperation with other children, anger/aggression, and anxiety/withdrawal. It can be completed by parents and/or teachers in about five minutes. More information can be obtained from www.wpspublish.com.

- Emotion Regulation Checklist (ERC) (Shields & Cicchetti, 1997, 1998): The ERC measures emotional expressiveness and regulation, and consists of two subscales: Emotion Regulation and Negativity/Lability. The Emotion Regulation subscale measures situationally appropriate emotional displays, empathy, and emotional self-awareness (e.g., "Displays appropriate negative affect in response to hostile, aggressive or intrusive play"). The Negativity/

Lability subscale measures the child's propensity to become distressed, including mood swings, angry reactivity, emotional intensity, and dysregulated positive emotions (e.g., "Exhibits wide mood swings," "Is easily frustrated"). The ERC can be completed by parents or teachers in five to ten minutes.

- Stress Survey Schedule for Persons with Autism and other Developmental Disabilities (SSS) (Groden, Diller, Bausman, Velicer, Norman, & Cautela, 2001; Goodwin, Groden, Velicer, & Diller, 2007): The SSS is a checklist used to identify individual stressors for each child that can be used as target goals for STAMP and can aid in understanding the origins of specific emotions and behavior.

11

TROUBLESHOOTING

Children with Asperger's disorder and HFA targeted for this treatment will have inherent social skills deficits and emotion regulation difficulties. Therefore, the group setting may be experienced as aversive for some of the children. Provided below are some common problems that may be encountered and tips for troubleshooting.

1. Child appears anxious in the group (may go off alone, hide, cry, etc.): Give the parents an outline of the session in advance so they can prepare the child ahead of time. These children often do better when they know what to expect. If the child is also being seen individually, their therapist can prime them in the same way. Children should be praised and rewarded within the group when they participate.

2. Behavioral problems/disruptiveness in the group: If the child is aggressive, he or she must be removed for the safety of the group. However, all efforts should be made in advance to prevent behavior from escalating to aggression. For example, the therapist could put a reward system in place for the child, so the child can earn a "break" or some preferred activity (like jumping on a trampoline) after earning rewards for appropriate group behavior. Another option is to teach the child to ask for help or to ask for a break when feeling agitated. Also, if possible, it helps to have an assistant in the room who can redirect the child to appropriate behavior or take them out of the room, if needed.

3. Child talks excessively or interrupts often: It may help to give the child a small whiteboard to write on when they have something to say and then have him/her read it at an appropriate time.

4. Parent reports that the child will not practice the tools/skills at home: This is a problem with generalization. To help with transfer of skills it may help to have the parents enter the child session during snack time and allow the children to review the skills with the parent in the session. Then, it may be an easier transition for the child to work with the parent at home. It is also possible that the child is not motivated to complete the assignments. In this case, it is helpful to remind the parents to complete assignments only when the child is already

calm and try to incorporate child interests into the assignment. For example, if the child enjoys computers perhaps the assignment can be completed using the computer, or time on the computer can be used as a reward for completing the assignment. Finally, if the child is still resistant a reinforcement system can be put into place, where the child can earn tokens, prizes, or activities after completing the assignment. Reinforcements should be chosen that are known to be meaningful for the child.

12

OTHER PRACTICAL ISSUES

1. Room setup: The room should be arranged to include plenty of space for games. It is preferable to have one side of the room with a table that can be used for craft activities and snacks, and another side with open space to use for games, stories, and discussion. Children should be seated in chairs or in some other assigned space (e.g., a carpet square), so that they have a visual idea of where they should be sitting. Children should be seated in a semicircle in front of the lead therapist.

2. Therapist qualifications: STAMP was originally tested using therapists who were advanced, post-masters students in clinical psychology or master's level occupational therapists. Therapists participated in a two-day STAMP training session and were supervised and assessed weekly to maintain fidelity throughout the efficacy test. This manual was developed, however, so that anyone can implement the program, regardless of their level of training or their specific discipline (e.g., psychologists, occupational therapists, speech therapists, general or special education teachers, counselors, etc.). Nonetheless, it is recommended that the person implementing the program has a good working knowledge about how to work effectively with children and about the characteristics of ASD.

3. Therapist number: The program is designed to have two adults in the room with the children, although it can be adapted to work with a single child and adult. In group settings, one adult serves as the lead therapist, and the second adult serves as an assistant to help keep children engaged or to troubleshoot problems that may arise during the session.

4. Use of rewards in session: As noted above, STAMP therapists are encouraged to use lots of praise, both verbal and non-verbal (e.g., high-fives, pats on the back), throughout the session. Therapists are also encouraged to maintain a positive atmosphere by using an enthusiastic tone of voice and smiling often. In addition to praise, stickers are provided to the children as a tangible reward for any demonstration of appropriate behavior (e.g., following the rules, completing homework, making an on-topic comment, etc.). The program

can be adapted so that stickers are provided immediately after each behavior and placed on a chart, or praise is provided immediately but stickers get distributed during review at the end of the session. We have seen both styles work in this program. However, for children with high anxiety/avoidance, attentional difficulties, or hyperactivity, a frequent schedule of reinforcement is often recommended. In these cases, it is best to provide immediate feedback through use of points, stars, or tokens that can be swapped for stickers later in the session. Either way, we recommend that stickers be distributed liberally to encourage and maintain desired behavior. Each session ends with a snack time, during which the therapist reviews the sticker chart for that session. Children are told that if they earn enough stickers they can have a group party at the end of the program, so that obtaining stickers has the potential to benefit both the group and the individual.

13
LIST OF RECOMMENDED MATERIALS

Core Materials

- See Appendix A: Children's Stories Used in STAMP
- Butcher paper on easel or whiteboard with markers and eraser
- Carpet squares or chairs for sitting
- CD player
- Certificates
- Children's magazines
- Crayons or colored pencils
- Digital camera
- Video camera (for fidelity checks and Session 9 video)
- Fun music CD
- Glue sticks
- Handheld mirror
- Index cards
- Velcro, tape, or glue stick
- Laminator
- Laminated pocket-sized cards
- Puppets
- Shoebox
- Stickers

- Sticky notes (Post-its)
- Playing cards or Go Fish cards
- Several poster boards
  - Poster board for sticker chart
  - Poster board or construction paper for collage
  - Poster board with a ruler drawn on it and Velcro
  - Poster board with photos of each child
  - Poster board with schedule and Velcro arrow
  - Poster with words to welcome song
  - Poster boards (one red and one green) for right tools (green poster) and wrong tools (red poster)

Ancillary materials

- Toy microphone (optional)
- Snacks from home
- Key rings (optional) for the index cards
- Heart rate monitor(s)

Note: Appendix A contains recommended books to be purchased before implementing the therapy. All books can be purchased through popular booksellers, such as Barnes and Noble, Amazon, and Borders. Other books can be substituted; however, they should be reviewed to ensure suitability for developmental level and session topics.

REFERENCES

Aman, M.G., Singh, N.N., Stewart, A.W., & Field, C.J. (1985). The Aberrant Behavior Checklist: A behavior rating scale for the assessment of treatment effects. *American Journal of Mental Deficiency, 89*, 485–491.

American Psychiatric Association (1994). *Diagnostic and Statistical Manual of Mental Disorders (4th ed.).* Washington, DC: American Psychiatric Association.

American Psychiatric Association (2000). *Diagnostic and Statistical Manual of Mental Disorders (Revised 4th ed.).* Washington DC: American Psychiatric Association.

Asperger, H. (1944). Die "autistichen Psychopathen" im Kindersalter. *Archive fur Psychiatrie und Nervenkrnkheiten, 117*, 76–136.

Baron-Cohen, S., Leslie, A.M., & Frith, U. (1985). Does the autistic child have a "theory of mind?" *Cognition, 21*, 37–46.

Centers for Disease Control and Prevention (2012). Prevalence of autism spectrum disorders. *Morbidity and Mortality Weekly Report Surveillance Summary, 61(SS03)*, 1–19.

Goodwin, M.S., Groden, J., Velicer, W.F., & Diller, A. (2007). Brief report: Validating the Stress Survey Schedule for Persons with Autism and Other Developmental Disabilities. *Focus on Autism and Other Developmental Disabilities, 22*, 183–189.

Gillott, A., Furniss, F., & Walter, A. (2001). Anxiety in high-functioning children with autism. *Autism, 5(3)*, 277–286.

Groden, J., Diller, A., Bausman, M., Velicer, W., Norman, G., & Cautela, J. (2001). The development of a Stress Survey Schedule for Persons with Autism and Other Developmental Disabilities. *Journal of Autism and Developmental Disorders, 31(2)*, 207–217.

Hill, E., Berthoz, S., & Frith, U. (2004). Brief report: Cognitive processing of own emotions in individuals with autistic spectrum disorder and in their relatives. *Journal of Autism and Developmental Disorders, 34(2)*, 229–235.

Kanner, L. (1943). Autistic disturbances of affective contact. *Nervous Child, 2*, 217–250.

Kim, J.A., Szatmari, P., Bryson, S.E., Streiner, D.L., & Wilson, F.J. (2000). The prevalence of anxiety and mood problems among children with autism and Asperger syndrome. *Autism, 4(2)*, 117–132.

Klin, A., McPartland, J., & Volkmar, F.R. (2005). Asperger syndrome. In F.R. Volkmar, R. Paul, A. Klin., & D. Cohen (Eds.), *Handbook of Autism and Pervasive Developmental Disorders* (pp. 88–125). Hoboken, NJ: Wiley.

Kopp, C.B. (1982). Antecedents of self-regulation: A developmental perspective. *Developmental Psychology, 18(2)*, 199–214.

LaFreniere, P. J., & Dumas, J. E. (1996). Social competence and behavior evaluation in children ages 3 to 6 years: The short form (SCBE-30). *Psychological Assessment, 4*, 442–450.

Ozonoff, S., South, M., & Miller, J.N. (2000). DSM-IV defined Asperger syndrome: Cognitive, behavioral, and early history differentiation from high-functioning autism. *Autism, 4(1)*, 29–46.

Scarpa, A., & Reyes, N. (2011). Improving emotion regulation with CBT in young children with high functioning autism spectrum disorders: A pilot study. *Behavioural and Cognitive Psychotherapy, 39*, 495–500.

Shields, A.M., & Cicchetti, D. (1997). Emotion regulation among school age children: The development and validation of a new criterion Q-sort scale. *Developmental Psychology, 33*, 906–916.

Shields, A., & Cicchetti, D. (1998). Reactive aggression among maltreated children: The contributions of attention and emotion dysregulation. *Journal of Clinical Child Psychology, 27*, 381–395.

Spence, S.H., Rapee, R.M., McDonald, C., & Ingram, M. (2001). The structure of anxiety symptoms among pre-schoolers. *Behaviour Research and Therapy, 39*, 1293–1316.

Sofronoff, K., Attwood, T., & Hinton, S. (2005). A randomized control trial of CBT intervention for anxiety in children with Asperger syndrome. *Journal of Child Psychology and Psychiatry, 46*, 1152–1160.

Sofronoff, K., Attwood, T., Hinton, S., & Levin, I. (2007). A randomized controlled trial of cognitive behavioural intervention for anger management in children diagnosed with Asperger syndrome. *Journal of Autism and Developmental Disorders, 46*, 1152–1160.

Tonge, B.J., Brereton, A.V., Gray, K.M., & Einfeld, S.L. (1999). Behavioral and emotional disturbance in high-functioning autism and Asperger syndrome. *Autism, 3(2)*, 117–130.

PART 3

Sessions and Resources

STAMP GROUP SESSION 1
EXPLORING POSITIVE FEELINGS (HAPPINESS)

The primary goal for the first few sessions is to introduce different feelings. Today we will be talking about feeling happy. There are different degrees of feeling happy. The Singing and Story Time Activities are used to prime the children for thinking about happy feelings. The Ruler Game is designed to explore degrees of happiness.

1. Cool Down

Time

10 minutes

Supplies

- Carpet squares or chairs for sitting on
- Butcher paper on easel or whiteboard with markers for rules
- Eraser for whiteboard (mitten eraser works well for children)
- Poster board with schedule and Velcro arrow
- Poster board for sticker chart

Schedule/Activity

Everyone relaxes with a cool down. Say to the children:

> The first thing we will do every week is cool down with a stretch and deep breathing. So, everyone stand up and reach to the sky like you are reaching to the sun. Now, try to catch some butterflies with one arm, then the other. Now, scoop down and pick up some flowers. Bring them up to your nose and sniff them with a deep long breath. Great job!

> Now that we're cooled down, let's sit back on our carpet squares (or chairs) and go over the group rules.

Tell the children the rules of the group and explain the schedule. The rules will involve the following:

- sit (in your seats or carpet squares)
- look (at the speaker)

- listen (to the speaker)
- calm voices/nice words
- nice hands.

The schedule will always be:

1. Cool Down
2. Welcome
3. Singing
4. Story
5. Activity/Game
6. Snack/Stickers and Goodbyes

Tell the children:

> Every time you follow the rules or use the tools we teach you in this group, you can earn a star (or token, point, etc.) and swap them for stickers at the end. If we earn enough stickers, we can have a big reward when the class is over in a few weeks. What would you like your group to work for if you get enough stickers?

Create a group end of program reward. The group members will suggest ideas that the entire group will work towards as reward for obtaining enough stickers at the program (e.g., if the group earns enough stickers, they can have a party).

Each child can earn a sticker for each rule followed, plus other stickers for effort/good behavior during the session. The stickers can be provided immediately after each behavior throughout the session, or you can distribute them at the end of the session, depending on the fit with the group members. It is also fine to provide differential reinforcement with stickers, such that a child earns a smaller sticker for doing a good job with the rule, but can earn a big sticker if they do a fantastic job. Since they are also working towards a group reward, each individual has a goal to do their best to "follow the rules and use their tools" during the individual session, but they are also working as a group for an overall goal. After describing how the stickers will be used, ask the children:

> Are the stickers good for you, or for everyone?

The answer is "both" because they will each get stickers, but the entire group can earn the reward at the end of the program.

2. Welcome

Time

10 minutes

Supplies

- Butcher paper/whiteboard with markers for noting each child's information
- Digital camera
- Handheld mirror (optional)

Schedule/Activity

Say to the children:

💬 Now it is time for us all to find out about each other!

Introductions—ask each child to tell the group about the following things:

- name
- age
- siblings
- pets
- favorite food
- "Where would you like to go for fun with your family?"

Note: Not all of these topics need to be covered if time is running short.

Take a picture of each person with a happy face. These pictures will be used to make a collage of happy faces. The group will welcome each person with enthusiasm at the beginning of each session. This sets the tone of each session. Since some children may be sensitive to having their picture taken, children can also draw pictures of faces or practice looking in the mirror and making happy faces.

Save copies of these photos for use in Session 8.

3. Singing

Time

5 minutes

Supplies

- Song written on poster with visuals
- Whiteboard or butcher paper to write reasons for understanding and managing our feelings
- CD of the song If You're Happy and You Know It to sing along with and CD player (optional)

Schedule/Activity

Ask the children:

💬 Does everyone know why we are here? In this group, we are going to be explorers who explore different feelings. What is an explorer? An explorer is someone who searches out new things and tries to learn about them. So, we are going to be explorers of our feelings to learn how to manage them. Why do you think we would want to understand and learn how to manage our feelings? What would be good about staying calm?

Get some ideas from the children, but guide them towards the following four reasons:

- to feel better
- to think better
- to stay out of trouble
- to make and keep friends.

After this session, create a poster with these four reasons to post on the wall for all future sessions.

Tell the children:

> Today we are going to explore the feeling of being happy. To get us in the mood, let's sing the song "If you're happy and you know it."

Sing the song with the following words: If you're happy and you know it, clap your hands (repeat). If you're happy and you know it, then your face will surely show it… If you're happy and you know it clap your hands. (Then repeat with "stomp your feet" and "shout hooray.")

Hold up the poster with visual aids so the children can follow along. Make a game out of it to see "Who can clap, stomp, or shout the loudest?" You can repeat the song several times, if time allows.

Having a CD of the song and words written on a poster board is helpful for the children to follow along with.

4. Story/Discussion

Time

15 minutes

Supplies

- Book
- List of discussion questions with visuals
- Butcher paper/whiteboard and markers
- Handheld mirror

Schedule/Activity

Read a story about happy feelings (e.g., *Mr. Happy* by Roger Hargreaves or *If You're Happy and You Know It* by Jane Cabrera). Explain to the children:

> Our feelings change all the time. One feeling that most people like is feeling happy. So, let's explore the feeling of happiness.

Present each of the following questions on a card with a visual aid clue to the answer. Using butcher paper or on a whiteboard, write each child's name at the top of the column and their answers for all to see. You can also draw a figure when appropriate or illustrate their responses (like jumping up for energy).

- When do you feel very happy?
- How do we know when we are happy?
- How does your face look? (look in handheld mirror)
- What thoughts do you have? / Do you feel *friendly*?
- How are your energy levels? / Do you feel you have the *energy* to do things you want?
- How do you move your body? / Do you feel *light* or *heavy*?
- How does your voice change?

The main point to get across to the children is that their thoughts are friendly and their body feels energetic and light when they are happy. Also, point out how their faces change when they are happy (e.g., smiling).

5. Ruler Game about Happy Feelings with Musical Chairs

Time

15 minutes

Supplies

- Poster board with a ruler drawn on it and Velcro
- Carpet squares/chairs
- CD player
- Fun music CD
- Happy words on index cards (shaped like leaves) with Velcro backing
- Happy situations on cards with Velcro backing

Schedule/Activity

For this exercise, draw a ruler or thermometer on a large poster board. Place two Velcro strips up it, about 6–12 inches apart. On one side of the Velcro, place ten tick marks, with the following labels stuck to each anchor:

- 1—a little happy
- 3—a little more happy
- 5—medium happy
- 7—very happy
- 10—very, very happy

Note: Use Velcro to label the anchors because you will use this same ruler again next week with angry/anxious feelings instead. Also draw dark circles to represent each anchor visually (e.g., five circles for medium happy, 7 circles for very happy, etc.).

Say to the children:

> Here is a ruler that goes from one to ten. It shows how our feelings might go from feeling just a little bit happy (one) all the way up to feeling very, very happy (ten), and our feelings can also go anywhere in between. This is called having different levels of happiness. We are going to play a game to teach us about how we might feel different levels of happy.

Play musical chairs, with just enough chairs for all the children minus one. Play music and the child left standing after it stops gets to place a happy card on the ruler. The cards will be words reflecting varying degrees of happy (with a picture that visually depicts the word), and the children must place it where they think that level of happy would be on the ruler. Keep playing until all the children have had a turn. Help them note how the numbers go up as they feel more happy.

Happy words list:

- Happy
- Proud
- Thrilled
- Excited
- Pleased
- Satisfied
- Ecstatic

Note: Some children will not know the meaning or nuances of all these words. If they do not seem to understand, you can teach them the definitions and show them where the words would go on the ruler.

In the next part of the activity the children should take turns to place situations along the ruler to reflect a degree of happiness (but without playing the musical chairs game). Before starting, ask the children what kinds of things make them really happy and place these things high on the ruler. Then ask them what kinds of things do not make them happy, and place them low on the ruler. Then say:

💬 Now, we are going to take turns trying to find things that fall in between these very low and very high levels of happy feelings. When it is your turn, you will get to pick a card and tell us where on the ruler would that situation be for you.

Example situations:

- Someone gives you a new tricycle or bicycle.
- You are eating cereal you like.
- You found your sneakers.
- Your brother turns on your favorite TV show.
- You are eating your favorite breakfast.
- Your teacher told you that you did good work.
- You just won your favorite game.
- Your mother says she loves you.

Note: The games in this manual are meant as suggestions and can be modified or substituted with other games as needed, as long as they are developmentally appropriate. For example, musical chairs may not be appropriate if there are fewer than three children in the group. You may include the teachers in the game to increase the players, or another game may be substituted. For example, you can play freeze dance: play music and then stop it; when the music stops, the children must freeze; the first person to move can place the card on the ruler.

6. Snack/Stickers and Goodbyes

Time

5 minutes

Supplies

- Snacks from home
- Stickers and chart

Schedule/Activity

It's time for a snack. While children are snacking, briefly review the main lesson of the session. Then, count out their stickers with them. Explain that:

💬 If we get all our stickers for the session, we get another sticker as a bonus.

Before leaving, make sure that the children say goodbye to each other.

✓

EXPLORING POSITIVE FEELINGS (HAPPINESS)

The primary goal for the first few sessions is to introduce different feelings. Today we will be talking about feeling happy. There are different degrees of feeling happy. The Singing and Story Activities are used to prime the children for thinking about happy feelings. The Ruler Game is designed to explore degrees of happiness.

1. Cool Down

2. Welcome

3. Singing: If You're Happy and You Know It

4. Story/Discussion about the book: *Mr Happy* or *If You're Happy and You Know It*

5. Activity/Game: Ruler Game about Happy Feelings with Musical Chairs

   Happy words reviewed:

   ○ Happy

   ○ Proud

   ○ Thrilled

   ○ Excited

   ○ Pleased

   ○ Satisfied

   ○ Ecstatic

   Happy situations reviewed:

   ○ Someone gives you a new tricycle or bicycle.

   ○ You are eating cereal you like.

   ○ You found your sneakers.

   ○ Your brother turns on your favorite TV show.

   ○ You are eating your favorite breakfast.

   ○ Your teacher told you that you did good work.

   ○ You just won your favorite game.

   ○ Your mother says she loves you.

6. Snack/Stickers and Goodbyes

Copyright © Angela Scarpa, Anthony Wells and Tony Attwood 2013
The STAMP Treatment Manual

Home Projects

- Parents help children *find different pictures of happy faces* cut from magazines or coloring books. Collect enough so that you have examples of: 1—a little happy; 3—a little more happy; 5—medium happy; 7—very happy; 10—very, very happy. Attach a label and/or number of the degree of happiness on each. These will be reviewed during the next session.

- *Find a book from the local library that deals with feeling happy and read it with your child.* Remind them of what it feels like to be happy—high energy, light, friendly, smiling, good thoughts.

- *Find a folder or binder* to collect your handouts and homework each week. Please bring this folder with you to session each week to review and add new information.

Copyright © Angela Scarpa, Anthony Wells and Tony Attwood 2013

Exploring Positive Feelings (Relaxation) and Anger/Anxiety— Emotional Toolbox Introduction

The primary goal for the first few sessions is to introduce different moods and feelings. This session will focus on the feeling of being relaxed, but we will also introduce other feelings—anger and anxiety. The Singing and Story Activities are used to help the children start thinking about relaxation. The Body Trace Activity will help us learn about relaxation, and then we will contrast relaxed feelings with angry and anxious feelings. The "emotional toolbox" of options for when we are feeling angry or anxious will be introduced.

1. Cool Down

Time
2 minutes

Supplies
- Carpet squares/chairs
- Poster board with schedule and Velcro arrow
- Poster board with rules
- Sticker chart

Schedule/Activity

Everyone relaxes with a cool down (stretch and breathe) and then sits at their seat/carpet square.

    Review the rules for group and remind the children that they can earn stickers if they "follow the rules and use their tools."

2. Welcome

Time

8 minutes

Supplies

- Poster board with photos of each child
- Poster with words to the Welcome Song
- Toy microphone (optional)
- Poster board with four reasons to stay calm

Schedule/Activity

Acknowledge and greet everyone by singing this Welcome Song to the tune of Where is Thumbkin? Teach the children the song by showing them words written on the poster board. If you have a toy microphone, hold it up to each child when it is their time to respond. Otherwise, point to the child to indicate their turn. Teach the children the following:

Group: Where is (child's name)? Where is (child's name)? [*Point to photo on poster board.*]

Child: Here I am! Here I am!

Group: How are you today sir/ma'am?

Child: Very well I thank you.

Group: We're glad you're here. We're glad you're here. [*Repeat for each child.*]

Review session from last week (feeling happy) and remind children of the four reasons we want to stay calm (i.e., to feel better, to think better, to stay out of trouble, and to make and keep friends). Refer to poster that has the four reasons listed.

Review home projects (different degrees of happy faces).

3. Singing

Time

5 minutes

Supplies

- Song written on poster board
- Song on CD (optional)
- CD player (optional)

Schedule/Activity

Sing the song with the following words: If you're happy and you know it, clap your hands (repeat). If you're happy and you know it, then your face will surely show it…if you're happy and you know it clap your hands. (Then repeat with "stomp your feet" and "shout hooray.") Having a CD of the song and words written on a poster board is helpful for the children to follow along with.

4. Story/Discussion

Time

15 minutes

Supplies

- Book
- List of discussion questions with visuals on cards
- Angry/anxious cards with visual answers to questions
- Butcher paper to list replies

Schedule/Activity

Say to the children:

> Last week we explored a feeling people enjoy—happiness. Today we are going to explore another feeling that people like—relaxation. Other words people use to say they are feeling relaxed are "calm, cool, rested, safe, comfortable, peaceful, and quiet."

Read a story about relaxation (e.g., *A Boy and a Bear* by Lori Lite or *A Boy and a Turtle* by Lori Lite).

Ask the children how their bodies show they are feeling relaxed. Then show each of the following questions on cards for the children to see. List their replies on the board.

- What happens to your heart?
- What happens to your breathing?
- What happens to your muscles?
- What happens to your face?
- What happens to your thinking?

Say to the children:

> Happiness and relaxation are feelings that people like. But we all know that sometimes people feel things they don't like—like feeling angry or anxious. Other words people use to say they are angry are "mad, annoyed, upset, or furious." Other words for anxious are "scared, afraid, or worried." These are very different from feeling relaxed.

Ask the children:

> How does your body show that you are angry? Or anxious? [*Again, have pictures on cards that illustrate some answers to aid the children (e.g., a hot face, a heart pounding).*]

5a. Body Trace Activity about Relaxed and Angry/Anxious Feelings

Time

15 minutes

Supplies

- Butcher paper for tracing
- Crayons/colored pencils
- One set per child of anger/anxiety signs on slips of paper (choose the first ten and any others known to be relevant for these children)

Schedule/Activity

Trace the outline of the children's bodies on paper. The children should then color/shade the areas on the body trace where they feel relaxation. This should take no more than seven and a half minutes. The remaining time is to contrast this with how their body feels when they are angry or anxious. Give each child a slip of paper with signs or clues that they may be feeling angry or anxious. Ask the children to place the paper in the area of the body where they may feel this.

Examples of signs include:

- increased heart beat
- fast breathing
- muscles tense
- making a fist
- red face
- frowning
- shaky voice
- loud voice
- crying
- thinking of hurting someone

- sweaty palms
- lump in throat
- gritting teeth
- flappy hands
- headache
- itchy skin
- tingly tummy
- wobbly knees
- feeling dizzy
- jumping up and down

5b. The Emotional Toolbox Introduction

Time

10 minutes

Supplies

- Index cards with cool-down tools and a picture (hole-punch each card so they can be placed on a key ring to carry around)
- Shoeboxes for each child
- Sample shoebox that is decorated with tools inside
- Key rings (optional) for the index cards

Schedule/Activity

Say to the children:

 Just like we have a toolbox full of different tools to fix a broken toy, we could also imagine another kind of toolbox to fix some of our feelings. There could be different kinds of tools in your emotional toolbox. One kind of tool might be a hammer. A hammer is like a physical tool that uses lots of energy to fix a feeling. Another tool might be a brush that can brush away the dust. A brush is like a relaxation tool that can help you to stay calm. There are other kinds of tools to fix feelings, too, like social tools and thinking tools. We will talk about each kind of tool over the next few weeks. For now, here are some tools you might put in your toolbox to help fix when you are feeling angry or anxious, and instead try to help you feel more happy and relaxed. We will explore these a little right now, but we will talk more about these next week.

Give each child tools to "cool down" written on cards along with pictures of that activity or thing. The cards will be sent home in a shoebox, which the children can decorate to make their own toolbox for next session (see Resource 1 for pictures of tools that can be printed and placed on index cards). Show the children a sample decorated shoebox with tools inside, so that they can have an idea of the final product.

Explain to the children that these are all toolbox options for cooling down:

- take a break
- sit by yourself
- talk to someone
- stretch
- meditation
- deep breaths
- lemons (squeezing hands and letting go)
- count to ten
- exercise
- dancing
- ask for help
- think of fun things

Note: One option for flexibility is to review the emotional toolbox during snack time, especially if the children seem to be getting antsy or if time is getting short.

6. Snack/Stickers and Goodbyes

Time

5 minutes

Supplies

- Snacks from home
- Stickers and chart

Schedule/Activity

It's time for a snack. While children are snacking, briefly review the main lesson of the session. Then, count out their stickers with them. Explain that:

If we get all our stickers for the session, we get another sticker as a bonus.

Before leaving, make sure that the children say goodbye to each other.

Exploring Positive Feelings (Relaxation) and Anger/Anxiety—Emotional Toolbox Introduction

The primary goal for the first few sessions is to introduce different feelings. This session will focus on the feeling of being relaxed, but we will also introduce other feelings—anger and anxiety. The Singing and Story Activities are used to help the children start thinking about relaxation. The Body Trace Activity will help us learn about relaxation, and then we will contrast relaxed feelings with angry and anxious feelings. The Ruler Game, introduced last week, will help us explore degrees of anger/anxiety. The "emotional toolbox" of options for when we are feeling angry or anxious will be introduced.

1. Cool Down

2. Welcome

3. Singing: If You're Happy and You Know It

4. Story/Discussion about the book: *A Boy and a Bear* or *A Boy and a Turtle*

5. Activities/Games:

   ○ Body Trace Activity about Relaxed and Angry/Anxious Feelings

   ○ The Emotional Toolbox Introduction

The emotional toolbox consists of physical tools, relaxation tools, social tools, thinking tools, special interest tools, and other tools. These will be reviewed with you today (see Resource 2). The toolbox options for cooling down are:

○ take a break

○ sit by yourself

○ talk to someone

○ stretch

○ meditation

○ deep breaths

○ lemons (squeezing hands and then letting go)

○ count to ten

Copyright © Angela Scarpa, Anthony Wells and Tony Attwood 2013

✓

- ○ exercise
- ○ dancing
- ○ ask for help
- ○ think of fun things
6. Snack/Stickers and Goodbyes

Home Projects

- Your child will be given a list of index cards with different tools for calming down, sent home in a shoebox that will be his/her toolbox. During the upcoming week, *decorate the shoebox together* and discuss each of the tools you put inside. Also, help your child identify something else that particularly calms him/her down and that he/she could also include in the toolbox (e.g., favorite brush or toy). *Please bring this toolbox with you each session.*

Copyright © Angela Scarpa, Anthony Wells and Tony Attwood 2013
The STAMP Treatment Manual

TOOLS FOR EMOTIONAL TOOLBOX

Take a break	Sit by yourself
Talk to someone	Stretch
Meditation	Deep breaths
Lemons (squeezing hands and letting go)	Count to ten
Exercise	Dancing
Ask for help	Think of fun things

Copyright © Angela Scarpa, Anthony Wells and Tony Attwood 2013

REVIEW OF EMOTIONAL TOOLBOX

STAMP Introduction to the Emotional Toolbox • Physical tools • Relaxation tools • Social tools • Thinking tools • Special interest tools • Sensory tools • Other tools • Inappropriate tools	**Physical Tools** Anything that increases heart rate and releases energy • Physical exercise, walk, run, trampoline • Sports practice • Creative destruction (recycling) • Should last for at least 10 minutes
Relaxation Tools Something to tone down the energy • Music • Drawing • Solitude • Massage • Reading • Repetitive • Sleep • Muscle relaxation • Deep breathing	**Social Tools** Using other people to help manage one's own feelings • Find someone to help change the mood • Talk to a family member or friend • Talk to a pet • Help someone else • Being needed • Counselor or mentor/buddy

Source: Angela Scarpa

Copyright © Angela Scarpa, Anthony Wells and Tony Attwood 2013
The STAMP Treatment Manual

Thinking Tools

- Self-talk
  - ° "I can control my feelings."
  - ° "I can stay calm."
  - ° "I can use my emotional tooldbox."
- Counting
- Put the event in perspective

  - ° "This won't last forever."
  - ° "They did not mean to hurt my feelings."
- Think something good about self

Special Interest Tools

- Engaging in one's special interest
  - ° Collecting
  - ° Science
  - ° Sports
- Can be very powerful and soothing for kids with ASD
- But should be controlled or time-limited to avoid excessive use

Others Tools

- Enjoyable activities
- Encouragement
- Illustrations of advice or coping skills
- Humor
- Social Stories™/power cards
- Create a comfort kit
  - ° Earplugs
  - ° Bubblegum
  - ° Squishy ball
  - ° Bendable wire toy
  - ° Pad of paper/pen to write thoughts
  - ° Eucalyptus smelling salts
  - ° Water to cool hot face
  - ° Current book

Inappropriate Tools

- Hurting self (suicidal throughts or self-injury)
- Fights or damage
- Retaliation
- Retreating to fantasy world
- Drugs/alcohol
- Punishment
- Affection (if it makes person more angry)

Copyright © Angela Scarpa, Anthony Wells and Tony Attwood 2013

Exploring Anxiety and Anger, and Physical and Relaxation Tools

This session will continue to focus on anger, anxiety, and the emotional toolbox—our options for cooling down when we get angry or anxious. The Ruler Game, introduced in Session 1, will help us to explore degrees of anger/anxiety. We want to use our tools at lower levels before the feeling gets too strong. We will focus today specifically on physical tools that help us raise our heart rates and release energy, and relaxation tools that help us bring our heart rates and energy down and make us calm.

1. Cool Down

Time

2 minutes

Supplies

- Carpet squares/chairs
- Poster board with schedule and Velcro arrow
- Poster board with rules
- Sticker chart

Schedule/Activity

Everyone relaxes with a cool down (stretch and breathe) and then sits on a seat/carpet square.

Review the rules for group and remind the children that they can earn stickers if they "follow the rules and use their tools."

2. Welcome

Time

8 minutes

Supplies

- Poster board with photo of each child
- Poster with words to the Welcome Song
- Toy microphone (optional)
- Poster board(s) with list of tools (optional: you can have a separate poster for each category of tools)
- Poster board with four reasons to stay calm

Schedule/Activity

Acknowledge and greet everyone with the Welcome Song (see Session 2).

Review last week's session (feeling relaxed versus angry/anxious and the emotional toolbox with list of tools posted). See Resources 3–7 for a sample of pictures that can be used for a poster of tools. All toolbox tools are included, but you should present those discussed so far. This can also be used as other tools are introduced over future sessions.

Remind children of the four reasons we want to stay calm (i.e., to feel better, to think better, to stay out of trouble, and to make and keep friends). Refer to poster that has the four reasons listed.

Review home projects (homemade toolbox).

3. Singing

Time

5 minutes

Supplies

- Song typed on paper (hint: put one verse per page in large letters and hold up one page at a time for children to follow along)

Schedule/Activity

Say to the children:

So far, we've explored what it's like to feel happy and relaxed. Last week, we also explored what it's like to feel angry or anxious. Now, we are going to learn a song about feeling angry and some of the tools we can use to fix it. This is called the If I'm Angry and I Know It song.

Note: If anxiety is more relevant to the children use the If I'm Anxious and I Know It song instead, which just substitutes the word "angry" for "anxious."

Sing only the first three verses of the song, which will review the physical and relaxation tools. Sing those three verses all the way through and then repeat the first verse, pointing to the words on the board (see Resource 8 for complete song words). Each week you will add a verse with the new tool being taught in that lesson. Today, teach the children the first three verses. Have the new words in each verse highlighted/bolded for the children to see easily. Then, get the children to sing the first three verses, pausing between the first and second verse to say that now you will sing about "physical tools" that help us release energy…and then between the second and third verse "relaxation tools" that help calm us down. Repeat the first verse at the end. Since the song is getting longer, be sure to sing at a moderate pace.

> Verse 1: If I'm angry and I know it, *use my tools* (repeat). If I'm angry and I know it, I can use my tools to slow it. If I'm angry and I know it, *use my tools.*

> Verse 2: If I'm angry and I know it, *count and breathe* (repeat). If I'm angry and I know it, I can use my tools to slow it. If I'm angry and I know it, *count and breathe.*

> Verse 3: If I'm angry and I know it, *stretch and move* (repeat). If I'm angry and I know it, I can use my tools to slow it. If I'm angry and I know it, *stretch and move.*

> Repeat first verse.

4. Story/Discussion

Time
10 minutes

Supplies
- Book
- Butcher paper with two columns for relaxation and physical tools
- Poster board(s) with list of tools (optional: you can have a separate poster for each category of tools)

Schedule/Activity

Say to the children:

> Last week we explored a feeling people enjoy—relaxation. Today we are going to talk about how we might try to relax when we start to feel angry or anxious by using tools from our emotional toolbox. Here's a story about a child who got angry.

Read a story about anger or anxiety (e.g., *Knuffle Bunny: A Cautionary Tale* by Mo Willems or *The Chocolate Covered Cookie Tantrum* by Deborah Blumenthal).

Ask the children what the child in this story could do to cool down and what tools she could use when she is just a little bit angry.

Remind the children of some of the tools in their toolbox, like a hammer that releases energy or a brush that calms their energy down. Point them to the poster board with the list of tools. You can add tools to the list for each category, based on the parent handout for this session.

Ask the children:

> Which tools help to release energy by increasing your heart rate and breathing? Which tools help to bring your energy back down by slowing your heart rate and breathing?

Write their replies on a butcher paper hung on the wall, with two columns—one for physical tools with a picture of a hammer, one for relaxation tools with a picture of a brush. Let them know that there are also other tools that you will cover in other sessions, but today they will focus on relaxation and physical tools. Then, practice some of the physical and relaxation tools.

5a. Ruler Game with Angry and Anxious Situations

Time
10 minutes

Supplies
- Ruler poster from Session 1
- Index cards of angry and anxious situations with corresponding pictures
- Happy music CD
- CD player
- Chairs for musical chairs

Schedule/Activity

Hang up the ruler poster from Session 1, but with angry/anxious anchors instead of happy anchors. Give each child a situation from the Child Measure: What Makes You Angry? and Child Measure: What Makes You Anxious? questionnaires (Appendix C), written on index cards along with pictures (from a magazine or from the internet). Ask them to place it on the Velcro from "a little angry or anxious" to "very, very angry or anxious." Help the children note how the numbers increase when they feel more angry or anxious. Remind them that they might feel any of these levels from time to time, and it is easier to calm down when they are at the lower levels.

Do this activity while playing musical chairs, like in Session 1 (any child-friendly game or activity can be substituted, as long as it is appropriately paced).

5b. Body Activity about Physical and Relaxation Tools

Time
15–20 minutes

Supplies
- Heart rate monitor(s)
- Coloring sheet
- Colored pencils/crayons

Schedule/Activity

Say to the children:

> So, we want to learn to use our tools when our anger or anxiety is still low, before the feelings get too strong. Now we are going to practice some tools you can use. Remember when we colored parts of our bodies last week where we felt relaxed or angry or anxious? We can actually make those parts of our body become relaxed by using our tools! Let's see how that happens by watching our heart rates. We will place this monitor on you so you can see your own heart rate go faster or slower as you practice your physical and relaxation tools.

After children review the physical and relaxation tools, they should further explore physiological relaxation through the use of heart rate monitors (remember to ask parent permission if the monitor goes under any clothing). Specifically, the children should practice exerting themselves (e.g., jumping up and down, running in place, etc.) to increase their heart rates, then choose one of the toolbox strategies to lower their heart rates. Let them see the numbers go up and down on the monitor. Children should be taught how this activity is related to the Body Trace Activity.

To keep some children occupied while others are measuring their heart rate, ask them to color a picture of a body, coloring where there body might feel relaxed (see Resource 9). If more time is needed, you can also explore more situations from the Ruler Game.

Note: If a child refuses to wear the monitor, he/she can watch the other children and help them with their tools. Also, a therapist can wear the monitor to model the exercise for the children. If a heart rate monitor is not available, measuring pulse rate or listening to breathing is also acceptable. The point is to help the child become aware of their physical sensations when they increase (physical tools) and decrease (relaxation tools) their arousal, and to recognize the tools that help them to do this.

6. Snack/Stickers and Goodbyes

Time

5 minutes

Supplies

- Snacks from home
- Stickers and chart

Schedule/Activity

It's time for a snack. While children are snacking, briefly review the main lesson of the session. Then, count out their stickers with them. Explain that:

> If we get all our stickers for the session, we get another sticker as a bonus.

Before leaving, make sure that the children say goodbye to each other.

STAMP Group Session 3: Parent Handout

Exploring Anxiety and Anger, and Physical and Relaxation Tools

This session will continue to focus on anger, anxiety, and the emotional toolbox—our options for cooling down when we get angry or anxious. The Ruler Game, introduced in Session 1, will help us to explore degrees of anger/anxiety. We want to use our tools at lower levels before the feeling gets too strong. We will focus today specifically on physical tools that increase our heart rates and help us release energy, and relaxation tools that help us bring our heart rates and energy down and make us calm.

1. Cool Down

2. Welcome

3. Singing: If I'm Angry and I Know It or If I'm Anxious and I Know It

4. Story/Discussion about the book: *Knuffle Bunny: A Cautionary Tale* or *The Chocolate Covered Cookie Tantrum*

5. Activities/Games:

   ◦ Ruler Game with Angry and Anxious Situations

   ◦ Body Activity about Physical and Relaxation Tools

   After children review the physical and relaxation tools, they will further explore physiological relaxation through the use of heart rate monitors. Specifically, the children will practice exerting themselves (e.g., jumping up and down, running in place, etc.) to increase their heart rates, then they will choose one of the toolbox strategies to lower their heart rates. Children will be taught how this activity is related to the body trace activity from last week. The idea is to use the physical and relaxation tools to change those same areas of the body to either increase or decrease our energy.

6. Snack/Stickers and Goodbyes

Copyright © Angela Scarpa, Anthony Wells and Tony Attwood 2013
The STAMP Treatment Manual

✓

Home Projects

- During the coming week, *remind your child of the tools they can use* when becoming angry or tense—especially the relaxation tools of deep *breathing and counting*, and the physical tools of *stretching and exercising. Sing together the first three verses of If I'm Angry and I Know It or the If I'm Anxious and I Know It (see Resource 8).*

- Throughout the week, you can talk about the things located in the toolbox. *When your child is calm,* remind him/her of the options he/she can use when becoming angry or anxious. Set up a reward system to use every time your child practices a tool.

- Remind your child that there are different degrees of anger or anxiety and it is easier to calm down if they can catch themselves at the lower levels. *Using Resource 10 try to identify some of the different levels together this week, especially the lower levels.*

- *Practice at least two or three times when the child is not in crisis (while calm),* and then every so often when they are a little agitated. When they are calm, say: "Let's practice getting even *more* relaxed." When slightly agitated, say: "I really want to help you solve your problem, but I cannot help until you are calm/relaxed." In addition to the reward system you set up, remember to naturally reward your child as much as possible when he or she uses the tools to relax—try to give the child what they want if possible (or some reasonable compromise) just to reinforce using the appropriate tools rather than using tantrums.

- *Feel free for you and your child to add to the toolbox* other tools that are individual to your child (e.g., reading, reciting state capitals, etc.). Review these with your child.

Copyright © Angela Scarpa, Anthony Wells and Tony Attwood 2013
The STAMP Treatment Manual

PHYSICAL TOOLS

Copyright © Angela Scarpa, Anthony Wells and Tony Attwood 2013

✓

Resource 4

RELAXATION TOOLS

Copyright © Angela Scarpa, Anthony Wells and Tony Attwood 2013
The STAMP Treatment Manual

SOCIAL TOOLS

Copyright © Angela Scarpa, Anthony Wells and Tony Attwood 2013

✓

Resource 6

THINKING TOOLS

Copyright © Angela Scarpa, Anthony Wells and Tony Attwood 2013
The STAMP Treatment Manual

Resource 7
SPECIAL TOOLS

HA HA

Copyright © Angela Scarpa, Anthony Wells and Tony Attwood 2013

✔

IF I'M ANGRY AND I KNOW IT AND IF I'M ANXIOUS AND I KNOW IT SONGS

If I'm angry and I know it, use my tools.
If I'm angry and I know it, use my tools.
If I'm angry and I know it, I can use my tools to slow it,
If I'm angry and I know it, use my tools.

If I'm angry and I know it, *count and breathe.*
If I'm angry and I know it, *count and breathe.*
If I'm angry and I know it, I can use my tools to slow it,
If I'm angry and I know it, *count and breathe.*

If I'm angry and I know it, *stretch and move.*
If I'm angry and I know it, *stretch and move.*
If I'm angry and I know it, I can use my tools to slow it,
If I'm angry and I know it, *stretch and move.*

If I'm angry and I know it, *ask for help.*
If I'm angry and I know it, *ask for help.*
If I'm angry and I know it, I can use my tools to slow it,
If I'm angry and I know it, *ask for help.*

If I'm angry and I know it, *change my thoughts.*
If I'm angry and I know it, *change my thoughts.*
If I'm angry and I know it, I can use my tools to slow it,
If I'm angry and I know it, *change my thoughts.*

If I'm angry and I know it, *do special things.*
If I'm angry and I know it, *do special things.*
If I'm angry and I know it, I can use my tools to slow it,
If I'm angry and I know it, *do special things.*

Sooooooo…

If I'm angry and I know it, use my tools. (Yippee!)
If I'm angry and I know it, use my tools. (Yippee!)
If I'm angry and I know it, I can use my tools to slow it,
If I'm angry and I know it, use my tools. (Yippee!)

Copyright © Angela Scarpa, Anthony Wells and Tony Attwood 2013
The STAMP Treatment Manual

If I'm anxious and I know it, use my tools.
If I'm anxious and I know it, use my tools.
If I'm anxious and I know it, I can use my tools to slow it,
If I'm anxious and I know it, use my tools.

If I'm anxious and I know it, *count and breathe.*
If I'm anxious and I know it, *count and breathe.*
If I'm anxious and I know it, I can use my tools to slow it,
If I'm anxious and I know it, *count and breathe.*

If I'm anxious and I know it, *stretch and move.*
If I'm anxious and I know it, *stretch and move.*
If I'm anxious and I know it, I can use my tools to slow it,
If I'm anxious and I know it, *stretch and move.*

If I'm anxious and I know it, *ask for help.*
If I'm anxious and I know it, *ask for help.*
If I'm anxious and I know it, I can use my tools to slow it,
If I'm anxious and I know it, *ask for help.*

If I'm anxious and I know it, *change my thoughts.*
If I'm anxious and I know it, *change my thoughts.*
If I'm anxious and I know it, I can use my tools to slow it,
If I'm anxious and I know it, *change my thoughts.*

If I'm anxious and I know it, *do special things.*
If I'm anxious and I know it, *do special things.*
If I'm anxious and I know it, I can use my tools to slow it,
If I'm anxious and I know it, *do special things.*

Sooooooo…

If I'm anxious and I know it, use my tools. (Yippee!)
If I'm anxious and I know it, use my tools. (Yippee!)
If I'm anxious and I know it, I can use my tools to slow it,
If I'm anxious and I know it, use my tools. (Yippee!)

Source: Angela Scarpa

Copyright © Angela Scarpa, Anthony Wells and Tony Attwood 2013
The STAMP Treatment Manual

MY BODY

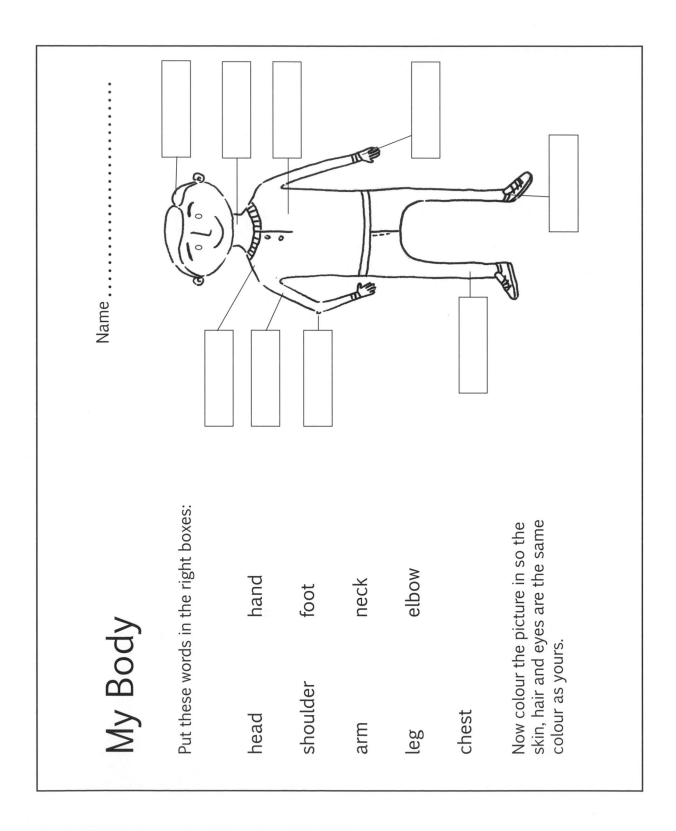

Copyright © Angela Scarpa, Anthony Wells and Tony Attwood 2013
The STAMP Treatment Manual

My Body

Put these words in the right boxes:

head   hand

shoulder   foot

arm   neck

leg   elbow

chest

Now colour the picture in so the skin, hair and eyes are the same colour as yours.

Name ....

Copyright © Angela Scarpa, Anthony Wells and Tony Attwood 2013
The STAMP Treatment Manual

✓

Resource 10

Exploring Anxiety and Anger, and Physical and Relaxation Tools—Home Project Resource

Child name: _____

These are times that I felt:

A little angry or anxious ★		
A little more angry or anxious ★★★		
Medium angry or anxious ★★★★★		
Very angry or anxious ★★★★★★★		
Very, very angry or anxious ★★★★★★★★★★		

Copyright © Angela Scarpa, Anthony Wells and Tony Attwood 2013
The STAMP Treatment Manual

SOCIAL TOOLS

This session will explore social tools to cool down. We will discuss how we can help others when they feel anxious or angry and how others can help us when we feel anxious or angry.

1. Cool Down

Time

2 minutes

Supplies

- Carpet squares/chairs
- Poster board with schedule and Velcro arrow
- Poster board with rules
- Sticker chart

Schedule/Activity

Everyone relaxes with a cool down (stretch and breathe) and then sits on a seat/carpet square.

Review the rules for the group and remind the children that they can earn stickers if they "follow the rules and use their tools."

2. Welcome

Time

8 minutes

Supplies

- Poster board with photo of each child
- Poster with words to the Welcome Song
- Toy microphone (optional)
- Poster board with list of tools
- Poster board with four reasons to stay calm

Schedule/Activity

Acknowledge and greet with the Welcome Song (see Session 2).

Review session from last week (physical and relaxation tools).

Remind children of the four reasons we want to stay calm (i.e., to feel better, to think better, to stay out of trouble, and to make and keep friends). Refer to the poster that has the four reasons listed.

Review home projects (practicing physical and relaxation tools and sheet of different degrees of feeling angry/anxious).

3. Singing

Time

5 minutes

Supplies

- Song typed on paper (hint: put one verse per page in large letters and hold up one page at a time for children to follow along)

Schedule/Activity

Say to the children:

Last week, we sang the If I'm Angry (or Anxious) and I Know It song. We sang about physical tools (stretching and moving) and relaxation tools (counting and breathing). Today, we are going to add social tools. Social tools are how others can help us cool down.

Teach the children Verse 4, which includes the phrase: "ask for help." Sing the verse once, and then sing it again with them. Then, sing the verses together from the beginning, pointing to the words on the board (see Resource 8). Have the new words in each verse highlighted/capitalized for the children to see easily.

Verse 1: If I'm angry and I know it, *use my tools* (repeat). If I'm angry and I know it, I can use my tools to slow it. If I'm angry and I know it, *use my tools.*

Verse 2: If I'm angry and I know it, *count and breathe* (repeat). If I'm angry and I know it, I can use my tools to slow it. If I'm angry and I know it, *count and breathe.*

Verse 3: If I'm angry and I know it, *stretch and move* (repeat). If I'm angry and I know it, I can use my tools to slow it. If I'm angry and I know it, *stretch and move.*

Verse 4: If I'm angry and I know it, *ask for help* (repeat). If I'm angry and I know it, I can use my tools to slow it. If I'm angry and I know, *ask for help.*

Repeat first verse.

4. Story/Discussion

Time
20 minutes

Supplies
- Book
- Butcher paper for listing social tools
- Poster board(s) with a list of tools
- Laminator
- Laminated pocket-sized cards with script

Schedule/Activity

Say to the children:

> Last week we explored using physical tools like exercise or relaxation tools like deep breathing. Today we are going to explore how we might use social tools, which means letting other people or friends help us to calm down. Here's a story about how a friend can help you feel better.

Read a story about friendship (e.g., *Otto Goes to the Beach* by Todd Parr).

At the end of the story, have the children repeat: "Sometimes, if I find a friend, I feel better!" Then move into a talk about social tools, and how sometimes we feel better if we let other people or even pets help us.

Ask the children to look at the list of tools posted on the hung poster and ask the following questions.

- Which tools might be social tools? (e.g., ask for help, talk to someone.)
- Can you think of any other kinds of social tools? (e.g., getting a hug, finding a friend, playing with pet, Mom/Dad saying "I love you.")

Teach them the following script to use when asking for help: "I feel _____ (sad, mad, worried, scared). Can you help me?" and "I have a problem. Can you help me?" Give them the script/s on a laminated pocket-sized card (see Resource 11) to hold and keep. Have the children put the card in their homemade toolbox.

Note: For less verbal children, the script can be changed to simpler language, such as: "Help please."

5. Social Play with Puppets

Time
20 minutes

Supplies
- Puppets
- List of discussion questions
- Butcher paper or whiteboard to write replies

Schedule/Activity

For this activity, use puppets (at least two) or dolls or other toys that may catch the children's attention (e.g., Transformers). Enact short stories using these puppets (see Resource 12). Use silly names for puppets, such as "Bonkers" or "Whazoo." The stories have different scenarios where a target puppet experiences being angry and anxious, respectively. To facilitate the understanding of social tools, the children should take turns coming up with ways that the other puppet could help the target puppet (the upset one) feel better. Another discussion can be started where the children are asked the following questions.

- What if it was you and your parent/brother/sister/friend/pet? How can they help you feel better?
- If your friend was angry like (the target puppet), how could you help them? What would you say? What would you do?
- If your brother or sister were feeling angry how could you help them?
- If your parent was feeling angry how could you help them?
- How could these people help *you*?
- Who could you talk to when you feel angry or upset (e.g., people or pets)?

If time permits, allow the children to enact a scene with the puppets, where they ask: "Can you help me?"

6. Snack/Stickers and Goodbyes

Time

5 minutes

Supplies

- Snacks from home
- Stickers and chart

Schedule/Activity

It's time for a snack. While children are snacking, briefly review the main lesson of the session. Then, count out their stickers with them. Explain that:

If we get all our stickers for the session, we get another sticker as a bonus.

Before leaving, make sure that the children say goodbye to each other.

STAMP Group Session 4: Parent Handout

SOCIAL TOOLS

This session will focus on using social tools to cool down. We will discuss how we can help others when they feel anxious or angry and how others can help us when we feel anxious or angry.

1. Cool Down

2. Welcome

3. Singing: If I'm Angry and I Know It or If I'm Anxious and I Know It

4. Story/Discussion about the book: *Otto Goes to the Beach*

5. Activities/Games: Social Play with Puppets

   ○ Learn the script for seeking help: "I feel (sad, mad, worried, scared, etc.). Can you help me?" or "I have a problem. Can you help me?"

   ○ Remember that most people respond to children's distress with affection, but some children with ASD do not like that; it's too intense. The way to handle this so the child can tolerate it is to *always* ask the child permission before giving affection. For example, "Is it OK if I give you a hug?" "Would you like me to stroke your arm?" "Can I take your hand?" If the child says "No," that's OK. It is fine to ask the child if there is another way you can help them.

   ○ Discussion: What are some ways of affection that your child can tolerate?

6. Snack/Stickers and Goodbyes

Home Projects

- Ask your child the following questions.

  ○ What tools do you like to use to calm down? Which are your favorite?

  ○ How can I help you out when you are angry or scared?

- Now, write those questions down for your child to read and ask you. *Answer with some tools you use and things they can do to help you when you are upset* (e.g., they can smile, offer help, give a hug, tell a joke, etc.).

- Practice using social tools with your child. *When they are getting upset, hand them their laminated card with script* and ask them to say: "I have a problem. Can you help me?" or "I feel _____. Can you help me?" Less verbal children can say, "Help, please." Have them say the script before you actually help them.

Copyright © Angela Scarpa, Anthony Wells and Tony Attwood 2013

Remind them that they can and should ask others for help whenever they are mad, sad, or scared.

- *Keep practicing* physical and relaxation tools. Remind them that you want to help them, but they need to be calm first. Continue rewarding children when they practice their tools.

Copyright © Angela Scarpa, Anthony Wells and Tony Attwood 2013
The STAMP Treatment Manual

Resource 11

Social Script Cards

I feel _____

(sad, mad, worried, scared).

Can you help me?

I have a problem.

Can you help me?

Copyright © Angela Scarpa, Anthony Wells and Tony Attwood 2013

Resource 12

Social Tools Stories

Whazoo Loses His Favorite Toy

One day, Whazoo and his friend Luna are playing at the park. They are having such a good time!

Whazoo: "This is so much fun, the swings are my favorite!"

Luna: "Oh, the merry-go-round is my favorite! But I really like being at the park with you because we are friends."

They both laugh. Then both children hear their parents calling. It's time to go home.

Luna: "Well, I'll see you next time. I had so much fun."

Whazoo: "I did too…wait a minute. Where is my toy?"

Luna: "I don't know where the toy is."

Whazoo becomes scared, his heart is beating fast, he feels shaky, and he begins to cry.

- How can Whazoo let Luna know how he needs help?
- How can Luna help Whazoo to not feel so scared?

Bubbles is Given the Wrong Cereal

One day, Bubbles and her brother Whazoo are with a babysitter while their parents are away. It's time for breakfast!

Bubbles: "I am very hungry and ready to eat!"

Whazoo: "Me too! I hope we are having cereal, I love cereal."

Bubbles: "Yeah, me too, especially Frosted Flakes."

Both of the children wait patiently. Then the babysitter gives them each a big bowl of Cheerios. Bubbles looks angry.

Whazoo: "What's wrong Bubbles?"

Bubbles: "This is not Frosted Flakes! I hate Cheerios. I want Frosted Flakes."

Copyright © Angela Scarpa, Anthony Wells and Tony Attwood 2013
The STAMP Treatment Manual

Bubbles can feel her heart beating fast, her muscles feel tight, her face turns red, and she begins to bang on the table, and scream in a loud voice, "I want Frosted Flakes!"

- How can Bubbles let Whazoo know she needs help?
- How can Whazoo help Bubbles to not feel so angry?

Ace and the Dentist

One day, Ace's mom was taking him to the dentist. Before they left, Ace began to get worried!

Ace: "Where are we going?"

Mom: "We are going to the dentist remember."

Ace: "Why do we have to go the dentist?"

Mom: "It is something we have to do to have healthy teeth."

Ace becomes scared, his heart is beating fast, he feels shaky, and he begins to cry.

- How can Ace let his mother know how he needs help?
- How can his mother help him to not feel so scared?

Goober and the Babysitter

One day, Goober's mom had to go to a special meeting while Goober stayed with the babysitter, Kiwi. While Goober's mom was getting ready, Kiwi arrived and mom opened the door.

Kiwi: "Hi Goober, how are you?"

Goober: "OK."

Goober gets butterflies in his tummy and feels shaky.

Goober: "Mom, don't go away!"

Kiwi: "But your mom has to go to her meeting Goobie."

- How can Goober let Kiwi know how he needs help?
- How can Kiwi help Goober to not feel so scared?

Copyright © Angela Scarpa, Anthony Wells and Tony Attwood 2013
The STAMP Treatment Manual

THINKING TOOLS

This session will focus on using thinking tools to cool down. We will explore how we can use thoughts to help us feel better when we become anxious or angry.

1. Cool Down

Time

2 minutes

Supplies

- Carpet squares/chairs
- Poster board with schedule and Velcro arrow
- Poster board with rules
- Sticker chart

Schedule/Activity

Everyone relaxes with a cool down (stretch and breathe) and then sits on a seat/carpet square.

Review the rules for group and remind the children that they can earn stickers if they "follow the rules and use their tools."

2. Welcome

Time

8 minutes

Supplies

- Poster board with photo of each child
- Poster with words to the Welcome Song
- Toy microphone (optional)
- Poster board(s) with list of tools
- Poster board with four reasons to stay calm

Schedule/Activity

Review last week's session (social tools) and, pull out and look at the social script(s) on last week's laminated cards from their home toolbox.

Remind children of the four reasons we want to stay calm (i.e., to feel better, to think better, to stay out of trouble, and to make and keep friends). Refer to poster that has the four reasons listed.

Review home projects (interview with parent about social tools). Ask the children:

💬 How can your mom or dad help you when you are feeling angry or anxious?

How can you help your mom or dad when *they* are feeling angry or anxious?

3. Singing

Time

5 minutes

Supplies

- Song typed on paper (hint: put one verse per page in large letters and hold up one page at a time for children to follow along)

Schedule/Activity

Say to the children:

💬 Last week, we sang the If I'm Angry (or Anxious) and I Know It song. We sang about physical tools (stretching and moving), relaxation tools (counting and breathing), and social tools (ask for help). Today, we are going to add thinking tools. Thinking tools are how we can change our thoughts to help ourselves cool down.

Teach the children Verse 5, which includes the phrase: "change my thoughts." Sing the verse once, and then sing it again with them. Then, sing the verses together from the beginning, pointing to the words on the board (see Resource 8). Have the new words in each verse highlighted/capitalized for the children to see easily.

💬 Verse 1: If I'm angry and I know it, *use my tools* (repeat). If I'm angry and I know it, I can use my tools to slow it. If I'm angry and I know it, *use my tools.*

Verse 2: If I'm angry and I know it, *count and breathe* (repeat). If I'm angry and I know it, I can use my tools to slow it. If I'm angry and I know it, *count and breathe.*

Verse 3: If I'm angry and I know it, *stretch and move* (repeat). If I'm angry and I know it, I can use my tools to slow it. If I'm angry and I know it, *stretch and move.*

Verse 4: If I'm angry and I know it, *ask for help* (repeat). If I'm angry and I know it, I can use my tools to slow it. If I'm angry and I know it, *ask for help.*

Verse 5: If I'm angry and I know it, *change my thoughts* (repeat). If I'm angry and I know it, I can use my tools to slow it. If I'm angry and I know it, *change my thoughts.*

Repeat first verse.

4. Story/Discussion

Time	*Supplies*
10 minutes	• Book
	• Butcher paper or whiteboard to list replies
	• Poster board(s) with list of tools

Schedule/Activity

Say to the children:

> Last week we explored social tools like talking to a friend or your mom, and asking for help. Today we are going to explore how we might use thinking tools, which means changing our own thoughts to ones that help ourselves to feel better.

Note: Therapists may need to explain what a thought is to the children. Ask them if anyone knows. If not, explain that thoughts are things we say or see in our own heads. They are ideas that we have. Tell the children:

> Here's a story about how Otto the dog changed his thoughts so that he could feel better.

Read a story about thinking (e.g., *Otto Goes to Bed* by Todd Parr). Point out that Otto is not really doing these things, he's just "thinking" them.

At the end of the story, have the children repeat: "Sometimes, I can change my thoughts to feel better." Then move into a talk about thinking tools, and how sometimes we feel better if we think about things differently—like thinking about fun things, things or people we like, or that we can control our own actions.

Ask the children to look at the list of tools on the poster and ask the following questions:

- Which tools might be thinking tools? (e.g., think of fun things to do.)
- Can you think of any other kinds of thinking tools? (e.g., thinking happy thoughts, thinking things are not so bad, thinking I can use my tools to stay calm.)

5. Thinking Game and Head Trace with Thought Bubbles

Time	*Supplies*
30 minutes	• Index cards with thoughts in a box
	• Butcher paper for head trace
	• Laminator
	• Index cards for thoughts/values
	• Ruler Game poster
	• Cards for the Big-Little Game

Schedule/Activity

Say to the children:

💬 Some thoughts we have can make us feel good, but other thoughts can make us feel bad by making us angry or anxious. Now, we are going to play a game to try to learn more about the kind of thoughts that may make us feel good or bad.

Duck, Duck, Goose Thinking Game: Get the children to play a game to explore different thoughts that may make them feel good or bad during times of anger or anxiety. Duck, Duck, Goose (or any other developmentally appropriate game), where the geese get to take turns pulling thoughts (written on index cards) from a box, is a good game. They must decide if the thought would make them feel good or bad. *If it would make them feel bad, ask the group how to change it to one that would make them feel good* (e.g., "Everyone hates me—but my mom loves me.") For all "feel bad" thoughts on the index cards, write on the opposite side of the card a corresponding "feel good" thought for the child to see.

The following thoughts can be used for the game; "bad" thoughts are followed by a corresponding "good."

- I'm a loser. (I'm a winner!)
- They will laugh at me. (Maybe they think I'm funny.)
- I can stay calm.
- I'm not good at homework. (My mom or dad can help.)
- It's not about winning, it's about having fun.
- I can't do this. (I can ask someone to teach me.)
- Everyone hates me. (But my family loves me.)
- Relaxing makes me think better.
- I can try again next time.
- Good choice.
- No one can help me. (I can ask for help.)
- Relax. It's not that bad.

Big-Little Game: Next, do this activity with the group, while one child is working on the next activity with another therapist. Use imagery from a card game, like Go Fish or any other cards that have differing numbers on them. While playing the game, teach the children how to identify which number is bigger, and the card that is bigger gets to take the other one away. Describe how your thoughts can work that way too. Explain that, for example:

💬 Now we know that sometimes we have thoughts that make us feel good, but sometimes we have thoughts that make us feel bad. These good and bad thoughts battle each other, kind of like our cards. The thought that is bigger can sometimes make the other thought go away. The trick is to figure out which good thoughts are bigger than our bad thoughts so we can think that good thought and feel good inside. Here's how to do that.

Direct one child to the other therapist for the next activity.

Note: If a card game seems too simple for your group of children, choose a special interest that is common to the group, like Transformers or Pokémon, to describe how the good and bad thoughts sometimes seem to battle one another. The stronger one wins, so we want to use the "feel good" thoughts that are stronger than the "feel bad" thoughts. Explain that, for example:

💬 Now we know that sometimes we have thoughts that make us feel good, but sometimes we have thoughts that make us feel bad. These good and bad thoughts battle each other, a bit like the Decepticons and Autobots in Transformers. The Decepticons are like the thoughts that make us feel bad, and the Autobots are like the thoughts battling to try to make us feel good. The trick is that the stronger thought wins, just like the stronger Transformer wins the battle. So, we want to figure out just how strong our bad thoughts are, so we can find a good thought that is even stronger. Here's how to do that.

Direct one child to the other therapist for the next activities.

Head Trace: Trace each child's head on a large piece of butcher paper and help them to identify one or two thoughts that make them feel good. Write the thought(s) in a bubble above their head trace.

Ruler Game: Then, pick a thought/situation that makes each child feel angry or anxious, either from your experience with the child, from parent-report, or from the Child Measure: What Makes You Angry? or Child Measure: What Makes You Anxious? questionnaires (Appendix C) completed before the program. Ask the child to assign a value to how strong the angry/anxious feeling is from one to ten (like the Ruler Game) and place that situation on the ruler. Then, help each child to identify a thought that would help them to feel good, along with its ruler value. The thought could come from the head trace or could be a new one that seems more appropriate. Remind them that the "feel good" thought needs to have a higher value than the "feel bad" thought, or the "feel bad" thought will not go away. Once identified, write the two thoughts and their values on an index card for them to take home and one for the therapists to keep. Have them put their copy in their home toolbox. Laminate your copy onto the side of a card (like a Go Fish card or Pokémon card) and give it to them next session as a gift.

6. Snack/Stickers and Goodbyes

Time

5 minutes

Supplies

- Snacks from home
- Stickers and chart

Schedule/Activity

It's time for a snack. While children are snacking, briefly review the main lesson of the session. Then, count out their stickers with them. Explain that:

💬 If we get all our stickers for the session, we get another sticker as a bonus.

Before leaving, make sure that the children say goodbye to each other.

In addition, review the good thoughts identified by each child and then *have the children practice saying their thought several times.*

STAMP Group Session 5: Parent Handout
THINKING TOOLS

This session will focus on using thinking tools to cool down. We will explore how we can use thoughts to help ourselves feel better when we become anxious or angry.

1. Cool Down

2. Welcome

3. Singing: If I'm Angry and I Know It or If I'm Anxious and I Know It

4. Story/Discussion about the book: *Otto Goes to Bed*

5. Activity/Game: Thinking Game and Head Trace with Thought Bubbles

   ○ For this activity we will trace the outline of each child's head onto paper. The children will play a game to decide on thoughts that would help someone feel better or worse. Then the children will write the words or strategies that they could say to themselves during times of anger and anxiety to help themselves feel better on to the head traces.

   ○ We will also teach you about thought bubble stories today, so you can create one with your child this week.

6. Snack/Stickers and Goodbyes

Home Projects

- Help your child practice using their thinking tools. Hang up their index card with their "feel good" thought. *When they are calm, ask them to repeat the thought.* Remember, it's best to practice several times when they are not in a crisis. After they seem confident with their thought, you can try practicing again when they are beginning to appear upset.

- Discuss different ways your child can use their thoughts to help them cool down with him or her. Some examples might include thinking:

  ○ of their pet

  ○ of a fun trip they took

  ○ of their favorite game

  ○ of visiting their grandparents,

  ○ that they can use their tools

  ○ it's OK to take turns, etc.

Copyright © Angela Scarpa, Anthony Wells and Tony Attwood 2013

- Together, note their "feel good" (helpful) and "feel bad" (not helpful) thoughts on Resource 13. Return the sheet next session.

- If your child becomes angry or anxious this week, help them write a thought bubble story about it. Wait till the child is calm (this could be even a day or more after the event), and then review the event with your child. On Resource 14, draw stick figures to represent the people involved in the event, and draw thought bubbles to reflect the thoughts your child was having that were not helpful or made them feel worse (e.g., "My mom never buys me anything"). If possible, also write what they thought the other person was thinking in the other person's thought bubble (e.g.,"I am never going to let him buy toys anymore"). Then, change the thought bubbles to more helpful thoughts in the next scene (e.g., "Maybe I can talk to Mom about buying the toy next time").

- Keep practicing physical, relaxation, and social tools. Remember to reward children for practicing and using their tools.

Copyright © Angela Scarpa, Anthony Wells and Tony Attwood 2013
The STAMP Treatment Manual

✓

Resource 13

GOOD AND BAD THOUGHTS

Feel-bad/not helpful thoughts	Feel-good/helpful thoughts

Copyright © Angela Scarpa, Anthony Wells and Tony Attwood 2013
The STAMP Treatment Manual

Resource 14

MY THINKING TOOLS STORY

Copyright © Angela Scarpa, Anthony Wells and Tony Attwood 2013
The STAMP Treatment Manual

STAMP GROUP SESSION 6
SPECIAL INTEREST TOOLS

This session will focus on using special tools to cool down. We will explore how each person has their own special way to make themselves feel better when they become anxious or angry.

1. Cool Down

Time

2 minutes

Supplies

- Carpet squares/chairs
- Poster board with schedule and Velcro arrow
- Poster board with rules
- Sticker chart

Schedule/Activity

Everyone relaxes with a cool down (stretch and breathe) and then sits on a seat/carpet square.

Review the rules for group and remind the children that they can earn stickers if they "follow the rules and use their tools."

2. Welcome

Time

8 minutes

Supplies

- Poster board with photo of each child
- Poster with words to the Welcome Song
- Toy microphone (optional)
- Poster board(s) with list of tools
- Poster board with four reasons to stay calm

Schedule/Activity

Acknowledge and greet everyone with the Welcome Song (see Session 2).

Remind children of the four reasons we want to stay calm (i.e., to feel better, to think better, to stay out of trouble, and to make and keep friends). Refer to the poster that has the four reasons listed.

Review last week's session (thinking tools)—from the home toolbox, pull out last week's thinking tool index card.

Review home projects:

- good/bad thoughts list
- social story with thought bubbles.

3. Singing

Time

5 minutes

Supplies

- Song typed on paper (hint: put one verse per page in large letters and hold up one page at a time for children to follow along)

Schedule/Activity

Say to the children:

Last week, we sang the If I'm Angry (or Anxious) and I Know It song. We sang about physical tools (stretching and moving), relaxation tools (counting and breathing), social tools (ask for help), and thinking tools (change my thoughts). Today, we are going to add special tools. Special tools are things we like to do that make us feel good.

Teach the children Verse 6, which includes the phrase: "do special things." Sing the verse once, and then sing it again with them. Then, sing the verses together from the beginning, pointing to the words on the board (see Resource 8). Have the new words in each verse highlighted/capitalized for the children to see easily.

Verse 1: If I'm angry and I know it, *use my tools* (repeat). If I'm angry and I know it, I can use my tools to slow it. If I'm angry and I know it, *use my tools.*

Verse 2: If I'm angry and I know it, *count and breathe* (repeat). If I'm angry and I know it, I can use my tools to slow it. If I'm angry and I know it, *count and breathe.*

Verse 3: If I'm angry and I know it, *stretch and move* (repeat). If I'm angry and I know it, I can use my tools to slow it. If I'm angry and I know it, *stretch and move.*

Verse 4: If I'm angry and I know it, *ask for help* (repeat). If I'm angry and I know it, I can use my tools to slow it. If I'm angry and I know it, *ask for help.*

Verse 5: If I'm angry and I know it, *change my thoughts* (repeat). If I'm angry and I know it, I can use my tools to slow it. If I'm angry and I know it, *change my thoughts.*

Verse 6: If I'm angry and I know it, *do special things* (repeat). If I'm angry and I know it, I can use my tools to slow it. If I'm angry and I know it, *do special things.*

Repeat first verse.

4. Story/Discussion

Time
15 minutes

Supplies
- Book
- Butcher paper or whiteboard to list replies

Schedule/Activity

Say to the children:

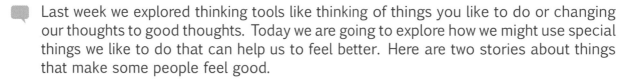 Last week we explored thinking tools like thinking of things you like to do or changing our thoughts to good thoughts. Today we are going to explore how we might use special things we like to do that can help us to feel better. Here are two stories about things that make some people feel good.

Read two stories about things that can make children feel good (e.g., *Things That Make You Feel Good, Things That Make You Feel Bad* and *Reading Makes You Feel Good* by Todd Parr).

Note: If other longer books are used, only one story needs to be read.

At the end of the story, have the children repeat: *"I can do a special thing to feel better."* Then move into a talk about special tools and how they can help us to feel good instead of feeling angry and anxious.

Ask the children what kinds of things they like to do that they really enjoy. For example, some kids like certain foods, games, pets, etc. Write their ideas down on the whiteboard or butcher paper.

5. Collage Activity

Time
25 minutes

Supplies
- Poster board or construction paper for collage
- Glue sticks
- Pre-made pictures of fun things (Resource 15, one set per child)
- Children's magazines

Schedule/Activity

Get the children to create their own collage by drawing and pasting on a half sheet of poster board (or on construction paper) special ways/interests that make them feel good or happy. Remind them that they can use these special tools to feel less anxious or angry. The following includes some ideas that can be suggested to the children to get them thinking about special tools they can use. Have pictures of each idea for the children to choose for their collage (one set provided for each child—see Resource 15). Quickly review each of these with the children by showing them the pictures and stating the activity. Although you can provide these ideas for the children, encourage them to come up with at least "one" special tool on their own. Other personalized ideas can be drawn or cut from magazines. The children can take their collage home to remind them of their special tools during the week.

- Some children use humor to feel better (simply recalling a humorous event or seeing the funny side can be a powerful tool).

- Some children act like someone they know who could cope well with the situation (e.g., a superhero).
- Some children listen to music to feel better.
- Some children do art or drawing to make them feel better.
- Some children go for a walk to make themselves feel better.
- Some children blow bubbles to help them feel better.
- Some children write about a problem to help them feel better.
- Some children ask their parents for a back rub.
- Some children pray to God to feel better.

After the collage activity, ask the children to practice saying: *"Sometimes, I can do a special thing to feel better!"*

6. Snack/Stickers and Goodbyes

Time

5 minutes

Supplies

- Snacks from home
- Stickers and chart

Schedule/Activity

It's time for a snack. While children are snacking, briefly review the main lesson of the session. Then, count out their stickers with them. Explain that:

If we get all our stickers for the session, we get another sticker as a bonus.

Before leaving, make sure that the children say goodbye to each other.

STAMP Group Session 6: Parent Handout
SPECIAL INTEREST TOOLS

This session will focus on using special tools to cool down. We will explore how each person has their own special way to make themselves feel better when they become anxious or angry.

1. Cool Down

2. Welcome

3. Singing: If I'm Angry and I Know It or If I'm Anxious and I Know It

4. Story/Discussion about the book: *Things That Make You Feel Good, Things That Make You Feel Bad* and *Reading Makes You Feel Good*

5. Activity/Game: Collage Activity

   o The children will create their own collage to take home about special ways/ interests that make them happy and that they can use to feel less anxious or angry.

   o Special tools are anything that is especially enjoyable for your child, including special interests or hobbies. Some examples are listed here.

   o Some children use humor to feel better (simply recalling a humorous event or seeing the funny side can be a powerful tool).

   o Some children act like someone they know who could cope well (e.g., a superhero).

   o Some children listen to music to feel better.

   o Some children do art or drawing to make them feel better.

   o Some children go for a walk to make themselves feel better.

   o Some children blow bubbles to help them feel better.

   o Some children write about a problem to help them feel better.

   o Some children ask their parents for a back rub.

   o Some children pray to God to feel better.

   o Any other special interest.

Copyright © Angela Scarpa, Anthony Wells and Tony Attwood 2013

✓

Note: Special interests can be very relaxing for children with ASD. However, the children can also get stuck on this activity. Therefore, it should be carefully monitored and time-limited. It may help to carry around a symbol or figurine of the child's special interest when you are out for times the child may be getting agitated. This may help be an "off-switch" for their anger.

6. Snack/Stickers and Goodbyes

Home Projects

- We have been teaching your child ways to categorize their emotional tools, such as relaxation tools, physical tools, social tools, and thinking tools, but you should explore with your child "special tools" that may not fit in these main categories. Examples include playing with toys, drawing, listening to music, or going for a walk, and often involve their own special interests. *Add these to your child's toolbox at home. Be sure to bring the toolbox to the next session, which will begin with a review.*

- Help your child practice using their special tools. *Hang up their collage where you can both see it.* When they are getting a little upset, show them their collage and ask them if they would like to do one of their special things *for a little while* to feel better. If they do, prompt them to ask you appropriately (so they are not reinforced for whining or other inappropriate behavior). Remember that you will need to limit their time if they tend to over-focus on this activity.

- *Keep practicing* physical, relaxation, social, and thinking tools, and reward children for practicing their tools.

Copyright © Angela Scarpa, Anthony Wells and Tony Attwood 2013
The STAMP Treatment Manual

PICTURES FOR FUN THINGS CHILDREN CAN DO

Some children use humor to feel better. 	Some children act like someone they know who could cope well with the situation. 
Some children do art or drawing to make them feel better. 	Some children go for a walk to make themselves feel better. 

Copyright © Angela Scarpa, Anthony Wells and Tony Attwood 2013

| Some children blow bubbles to help them feel better.  | Some children write about a problem to help them feel better.  |
| Some children ask their parents for a back rub.  | Some children pray to God to feel better.  |

Copyright © Angela Scarpa, Anthony Wells and Tony Attwood 2013
The STAMP Treatment Manual

APPROPRIATE AND INAPPROPRIATE TOOLS

This session will focus on understanding the difference between right ways (appropriate) and wrong ways (inappropriate) for cooling down. This also serves as an initial review of our emotional toolbox.

1. Cool Down

Time

2 minutes

Supplies

- Carpet squares/chairs
- Poster board with schedule and Velcro arrow
- Poster board with rules
- Sticker chart

Schedule/Activity

Everyone relaxes with a cool down (stretch and breathe) and then sits on a seat/carpet square.

Review the rules for group and remind the children that they can earn stickers if they "follow the rules and use their tools."

2. Welcome

Time

8 minutes

Supplies

- Poster board with photo of each child
- Poster with words to the Welcome Song posted
- Toy microphone (optional)
- Poster board(s) with list of tools
- Poster board with four reasons to stay calm

Schedule/Activity

Acknowledge and greet everyone with the Welcome Song (see Session 2).

Remind children of the four reasons we want to stay calm (i.e., to feel better, to think better, to stay out of trouble, and to make and keep friends). Refer to the poster that has the four reasons listed.

Review last week's session (special tools).

Review home projects:

- ask about and pull out any special tools added to home toolboxes

- review other tools in the toolbox.

3. Singing

Time

5 minutes

Supplies

- Song typed on paper (hint: put one verse per page in large letters and hold up one page at a time for children to follow along)

Schedule/Activity

Say to the children:

> Last week, we sang the If I'm Angry (or Anxious) and I Know It song. We sang about physical tools (stretching and moving), relaxation tools (counting and breathing), social tools (ask for help), thinking tools (change my thoughts), and special tools (do special things). Those are all the different kinds of tools we might use to fix our feelings if we are angry or anxious. Let's practice singing our whole song!

Sing all the verses together from the beginning, pointing to the words on the board (see Resource 8).

> Verse 1: If I'm angry and I know it, *use my tools* (repeat). If I'm angry and I know it, I can use my tools to slow it. If I'm angry and I know it, *use my tools.*
>
> Verse 2: If I'm angry and I know it, *count and breathe* (repeat). If I'm angry and I know it, I can use my tools to slow it. If I'm angry and I know it, *count and breathe.*
>
> Verse 3: If I'm angry and I know it, *stretch and move* (repeat). If I'm angry and I know it, I can use my tools to slow it. If I'm angry and I know it, *stretch and move.*
>
> Verse 4: If I'm angry and I know it, *ask for help* (repeat). If I'm angry and I know it, I can use my tools to slow it. If I'm angry and I know it, *ask for help.*
>
> Verse 5: If I'm angry and I know it, *change my thoughts* (repeat). If I'm angry and I know it, I can use my tools to slow it. If I'm angry and I know it, *change my thoughts.*
>
> Verse 6: If I'm angry and I know it, *do special things* (repeat). If I'm angry and I know it, I can use my tools to slow it. If I'm angry and I know it, *do special things.*
>
> Repeat first verse.

4. Story/Discussion

Time

15 minutes

Supplies

- Book
- Posters with tools listed
- One poster for each category of tools
- *The Social Skills Picture Book*

Schedule/Activity

Say to the children:

> In this group, we've been exploring our feelings and different tools we can use to help ourselves feel good if we are upset. Here's a story about a girl who didn't know about these tools. Let's see what happened.

Read a story about anger or anxiety (e.g., *The Chocolate Covered Cookie Tantrum* by Deborah Blumenthal or *Knuffle Bunny: A Cautionary Tale* by Mo Willems) where a child becomes noticeably upset. Be sure to use a different story from the one read in Session 3.

Ask the children the following questions:

- What are some different ways that (the main character) could have used to calm down? Give each child a poster with a category of tools and sample tools (with pictures) listed on each one (e.g., the physical tools poster would list/show jumping, exercising, sports, dancing, etc.). Ask each child to pick a tool on the poster that the character could have used.

- Have any of you ever had times when you cried or got really upset (had tantrums) like (the main character)? What did you do during those times? What made you feel worse? What made you feel better? Talk about how sometimes we use tools that make us feel worse—like screaming, crying, hitting. These are wrong tools because they do not help us feel calm. If we want to feel good, we need to think about the right tools to use.

- Why do we want to stay calm? Talk about how if we hit or yell we may lose friends or hurt others. Focus on friendship and consequences for using wrong tools versus right tools. Even words (like yelling or calling people names) can hurt others as much as hitting.

Read the Keeping Calm module from *The Social Skills Picture Book* by Jed Baker as a visual aid and introduction for the "right way" and the "wrong way" for cooling down.

5. Right versus Wrong Tools Game

Time

25 minutes

Supplies

- Two poster boards (one red and one green) for right (green poster) tools and wrong (red poster) tools
- Sticky notes with right and wrong tools listed
- Crayons/colored pencils and paper for "paper toolboxes" (optional scissors and glue)

Schedule/Activity

Ask children to place sticky notes with the "right way" and "wrong way" to cool down in the correct category (listed below). The activity should be played as a game where the children sit in a circle (similar to Duck, Duck, Goose) and the child who gets tapped gets to place the sticky note in the correct category on the corresponding poster board (red board for wrong tools and green board for right tools). Then discuss why some tools are a good idea (e.g., because we feel calmer, we can think better, we do not get into trouble, etc.) and others are not such a good idea (e.g., because we get more upset, others get hurt, etc.).

Right Tools versus Wrong Tools:

- Take a break/Hitting someone
- Sit by yourself/Spitting
- Talk to someone/ Crying
- Stretch/Hurting yourself
- Meditate/Thinking about something mean/bad
- Deep breaths/Making mean gestures
- Lemons/Having a meltdown
- Count to ten/Saying mean words
- Think of something happy/Screaming
- Do something fun/Kicking
- Cool down/Throwing things
- Go for a walk/Hiding

Making a Tool Chart: As a craft activity during the session, help the children to create their own chart to use during the week to monitor how they are using their tools. You can call this chart their own "paper toolbox" and cut it into the shape of a toolbox, or use the toolbox templates on Resource 16 and paste the chart on the back. If they draw their own chart in the session, the chart will have two columns, one for right/good tools and one for wrong/bad tools for calming down (see Resource 17). Color green above the column for right tools, and red above the column for wrong tools. During the week, the children need to keep track of the tools they used on this chart and if the tool was a right/good tool or wrong/bad tool for cooling down and feeling better.

Note: This last activity can go into snack time if time is running short.

6. Snack/Stickers and Goodbyes

Time

5 minutes

Supplies

- Snacks from home
- Stickers and chart

Schedule/Activity

It's time for a snack. While children are snacking, briefly review the main lesson of the session. Then, count out their stickers with them. Explain that:

💬 If we get all our stickers for the session, we get another sticker as a bonus.

Before leaving, make sure that the children say goodbye to each other.

STAMP Group Session 7: Parent Handout

APPROPRIATE AND INAPPROPRIATE TOOLS

This session will review tools we have learned for cooling down. Your child will leave today with an idea of tools that are appropriate ("right tools") or inappropriate ("wrong tools"). You can continue this discussion at home by talking about the specific ways your child uses to deal with anger or anxiety during the week.

1. Cool Down

2. Welcome

3. Singing: If I'm Angry and I Know It or If I'm Anxious and I Know It

4. Story/Discussion about the book: *The Chocolate Covered Cookie Tantrum* or *Knuffle Bunny: A Cautionary Tale*

5. Activity/Game: Right Tools versus Wrong Tools Game

   ◦ Which tools should we use?

Right tools	Wrong tools
Take a break	Hitting someone
Sit by yourself	Spitting
Talk to someone	Crying
Stretch	Hurting yourself
Meditate	Thinking about something mean/bad
Deep breaths	Making mean gestures
Lemons	Having a meltdown
Count to ten	Saying mean words
Think of something happy	Screaming
Do something fun	Kicking
Cool down	Throwing things
Go for a walk	Hiding

   Note: Sometimes children call names, yell, or use obscene language as a wrong tool. If this happens, give them a visual cue that you are hurt. Cover your ears as if in pain and say "Oh, those words hurt me," just as you might rub an arm or leg if it were hit.

   ◦ Making a Tool Chart

6. Snack/Stickers and Goodbyes

Copyright © Angela Scarpa, Anthony Wells and Tony Attwood 2013

✓

Home Projects

- After discussing "right tools" and "wrong tools" tools in today's session, we would like you to help your child keep track of which tools he or she actually uses at home. Your child will take home a chart of right tools/wrong tools (created in today's session) to return next session. During the week, *help your child record* on his or her tool chart any tools he or she used and if the tool is right (helpful) or wrong (unhelpful).

- Remind them that the right tools can be categorized as:

  ○ social tools (e.g., talk to someone)—these tools include the ways that other people can help fix angry or anxious feelings

  ○ thinking tools (e.g., think of something happy)—these are thoughts or ideas that can help us feel better

  ○ physical tools (e.g., exercising)—these are ways we use our body to help us feel better by releasing energy

  ○ relaxation tools (e.g., lemons, deep breathing)—these are things we do to calm our body and bring the energy down

  ○ special tools (e.g., go for a walk, favorite toy)—these are individual interests your child can use to feel better.

  When listing items on your child's tool chart, identify for your child the kind of tool it was.

- *Also record your own parent chart (Resource 18)*, which has more specific information that will help you track how things are working at home. On your parent chart, note the situation, a description of the tool, the kind of tool that was used, and any consequences. *Place a star next to those tools that you identified as "right" tools.*

Copyright © Angela Scarpa, Anthony Wells and Tony Attwood 2013
The STAMP Treatment Manual

Resource 16

TOOLBOX TEMPLATES

Copyright © Angela Scarpa, Anthony Wells and Tony Attwood 2013

Copyright © Angela Scarpa, Anthony Wells and Tony Attwood 2013
The STAMP Treatment Manual

✓

Resource 17
TOOL CHART

Right/Good Tools	Wrong/Bad Tools

Copyright © Angela Scarpa, Anthony Wells and Tony Attwood 2013

✓

Resource 18

PARENT CHART

Child's name: _____

Instructions: Please use this sheet to record the appropriate and inappropriate tools your child has used to cool down over the past week.

Situation	Tool used (add * if appropriate)	Kind of tool used (physical, relaxation, social, thinking, or special)	Consequences
Who? What? When? Why?			
Who? What? When? Why?			
Who? What? When? Why?			
Who? What? When? Why?			

Copyright © Angela Scarpa, Anthony Wells and Tony Attwood 2013
The STAMP Treatment Manual

REVIEW (GROUP STORY AND CREATE A COMMERCIAL)

This session will focus on reviewing all the tools we have learned.

1. Cool Down

Time	*Supplies*
2 minutes	• Carpet squares/chairs
	• Poster board with schedule and Velcro arrow
	• Poster board with rules
	• Sticker chart

Schedule/Activity

Everyone relaxes with a cool down (stretch and breathe) and then sits on a seat/carpet square.

Review the rules for group and remind the children that they can earn stickers if they "follow the rules and use their tools."

2. Welcome

Time	*Supplies*
8 minutes	• Poster board with photo of each child
	• Poster with words to the Welcome Song
	• Toy microphone (optional)
	• Poster board(s) with list of tools
	• Poster board with four reasons to stay calm

Schedule/Activity

Acknowledge and greet everyone with the Welcome Song (see Session 2).

Remind children of the four reasons we want to stay calm (i.e., to feel better, to think better, to stay out of trouble, and to make and keep friends). Refer to the poster that has the four reasons listed.

Review last week's session (right/wrong tools).

Review the child's chart of right/wrong tools they did as a home project.

3. Singing

Time

5 minutes

Supplies

- Song typed on paper (hint: put one verse per page in large letters and hold up one page at a time for children to follow along)

Schedule/Activity

Say to the children:

💬 Let's practice singing our whole If I'm Angry (or Anxious) and I Know It song!

Sing all the verses together from the beginning, pointing to the words on the paper (see Resource 8).

💬 Verse 1: If I'm angry and I know it, *use my tools* (repeat). If I'm angry and I know it, I can use my tools to slow it. If I'm angry and I know it, *use my tools.*

Verse 2: If I'm angry and I know it, *count and breathe* (repeat). If I'm angry and I know it, I can use my tools to slow it. If I'm angry and I know it, *count and breathe.*

Verse 3: If I'm angry and I know it, *stretch and move* (repeat). If I'm angry and I know it, I can use my tools to slow it. If I'm angry and I know it, *stretch and move.*

Verse 4: If I'm angry and I know it, *ask for help* (repeat). If I'm angry and I know it, I can use my tools to slow it. If I'm angry and I know it, *ask for help.*

Verse 5: If I'm angry and I know it, *change my thoughts* (repeat). If I'm angry and I know it, I can use my tools to slow it. If I'm angry and I know it, *change my thoughts.*

Verse 6: If I'm angry and I know it, *do special things* (repeat). If I'm angry and I know it, I can use my tools to slow it. If I'm angry and I know it, *do special things.*

Repeat first verse.

4. Story/Discussion

Time
15 minutes

Supplies
- Our Group Story

Schedule/Activity

Our Group Story: Before the session, create a story (see Resource 19) that uses each of the children as a character. Use a copy of the child's photo for their page in the story. Write the story so it reviews the tools covered. The story can go like this (but feel free to edit):

> Once upon a time, there were four children [*adapt to number of children in the group*] named (Child 1, Child 2, Child 3, and Child 4). The children loved to play together, but one day a wizard came to town and made all their toys disappear! They were angry, and they were scared. But, then they all came up with a plan to calm down and feel better. First, Child 1 said, "Let's use a physical tool to feel better!" So, they all played a game of chase to let out their energy. Then, Child 2 said, "Let's use a relaxation tool to calm down." So, they all practiced their deep breathing. [*Go through each set of tools in the story...*] At the end, they all felt better knowing they have each other and their tools.

Give each child a copy of the book to keep. If confidentiality is an issue, be sure to obtain permission from parents before distributing to other group members. If permission is not available, do not use the children's pictures or names in the story that is distributed.

5. Review Activities

Time
25 minutes

Supplies
- Poster board with tools listed
- Stickers
- Puppets
- Video camera

Schedule/Activity

Review with Home Toolboxes and Puppets: Have poster board(s) with all the tools listed (e.g., exercise, stretch, deep breaths, count to ten, etc.). Refer back to this poster while each child goes through their own homemade toolbox. Bring back the puppets Whazoo and Bubbles from Session 4. Have the puppets recap the original tools we provided and then ask the children the following questions.

- Did you add any other tools to your toolbox?
- Would you like to add any new tools now?
- Which tools do you find especially helpful for you to calm down or feel better?

Place a star sticker next to their favorite/most helpful tools.

Video Review (Create a Commercial): After identifying the tools they like the best, make a video of each child taking turns to talk about is or her favorite tools (about 30–60 seconds each). Say:

> 💬 We will be making a commercial of all the tools that you would like to remember.

Ask them which tools they would like to remember and then record them saying it and demonstrating it. They can choose more than one. The teacher(s) should also say and demonstrate a tool to include on the video, to ensure that there are a variety of tools captured. If time permits, the group can then sing the If I'm Angry (or Anxious) and I Know It song for the end of the commercial.

Note: If they do not know what to say, you can write it down for them in a script (e.g., "I can ask other people for help to feel better," "I can change my thoughts," "I can do special things"), or they can sing part of a song.

During the week, make a copy of the video for each child to take home at the final session so they will always be able to remember the group.

Note: If confidentiality is an issue, be sure to obtain permission from parents before distributing to other group members. If permission is not available, then do not merge the videos, and provide each child only with their own individual video.

6. Snack/Stickers and Goodbyes

Time

5 minutes

Supplies

- Snacks from home
- Stickers and chart

Schedule/Activity

It's time for a snack. While children are snacking, briefly review the main lesson of the session. Then, count out their stickers with them. Explain that:

> 💬 If we get all our stickers for the session, we get another sticker as a bonus.

Before leaving, make sure that the children say goodbye to each other.

STAMP Group Session 8: Parent Handout
Review (Group Story and Create a Commercial)

This session will focus on reviewing all the tools we have learned.

1. Cool Down

2. Welcome

3. Singing: If I'm Angry and I Know It or If I'm Anxious and I Know It

4. Story: *Our Group Story* (note: obtain parental permission before distributing story)

5. Activity/Game: Review activities

   ○ Review with Home Toolboxes and Puppets: The children will review all the tools in their toolboxes, and add more if they like.

   ○ Video Review/Create a Commercial: The children will make a video commercial of their favorite tools from their emotional toolbox. Next week we will review the video and provide a copy for each child to take home. (Note: Obtain parental permission to distribute videos for next session.)

6. Snack/Stickers and Goodbyes

Important: Next week will be our final session. We will watch our group video, complete final assessments, have a party, and distribute the videos and certificates of completion to each child.

Home Projects

• Together with your child, *review the items in your child's* home toolbox. Personalize the toolbox by adding any other tools/activities that your child finds helpful.

• Please *complete the seven behavior monitoring sheets (Resource 20)* (one per day, starting today), so that we can assess any changes over the course of the group. Please return this sheet next session.

• *Keep practicing and rewarding your child!*

Copyright © Angela Scarpa, Anthony Wells and Tony Attwood 2013

✓

SAMPLE FOR OUR GROUP STORY

Once upon a time, there were three children who really liked each other and liked to play together. Their names were Johnny, Billy, and Sally.

- Insert photographs of the children here.

Copyright © Angela Scarpa, Anthony Wells and Tony Attwood 2013
The STAMP Treatment Manual

One day, Ms. Johnson, Ms. Sanchez and Ms. Baker saw Johnny, Billy, and Sally playing together and sharing toys when, suddenly, a wizard came and took the children's toys away!

- Insert a picture of a wizard here.

Copyright © Angela Scarpa, Anthony Wells and Tony Attwood 2013

The children felt angry and they also felt scared because they could not play with their toys anymore, but then they remembered their tools!

- Insert faces with angry and anxious emotions here.

- Insert photographs of the children here.

Copyright © Angela Scarpa, Anthony Wells and Tony Attwood 2013
The STAMP Treatment Manual

Johnny said, "I am angry because the wizard took our toys away from us, but I am going to use a physical tool to feel better." Johnny started squeezing lemons, and that helped him to feel better!

- Insert a picture of the tool suggested here.

- Insert a photograph of Johnny here.

Copyright © Angela Scarpa, Anthony Wells and Tony Attwood 2013

Then, Billy said, "I also feel scared and anxious, but I am going to use a special tool to feel better." Billy decided to read his favorite book and he felt better!

- Insert a picture of the tool suggested here.

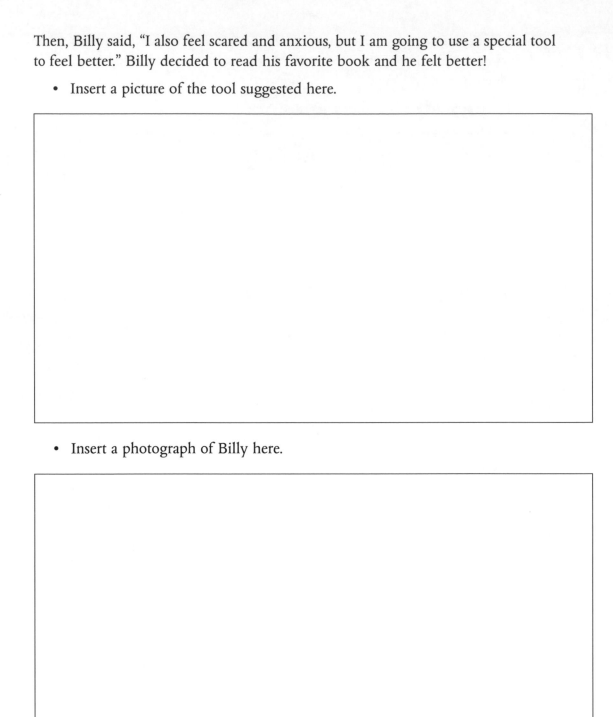

- Insert a photograph of Billy here.

Copyright © Angela Scarpa, Anthony Wells and Tony Attwood 2013
The STAMP Treatment Manual

Also, Sally said, "I am anxious too, but I am going to use a relaxation tool to feel better." She started breathing slowly and counting to ten and she felt better!

- Insert a picture of the tool suggested here.

- Insert a photograph of Sally here.

Copyright © Angela Scarpa, Anthony Wells and Tony Attwood 2013

Ms. Johnson also reminded the children that they could use a thinking tool, so the children started thinking happy thoughts to help them feel better.

- Insert a picture of the tool suggested here.

- Insert a photograph of Ms. Johnson here.

Copyright © Angela Scarpa, Anthony Wells and Tony Attwood 2013
The STAMP Treatment Manual

Ms. Sanchez told them that they could use a social tool, so the children decided to find an adult to help them.

- Insert a picture of the tool suggested here.

- Insert a photograph of Ms. Sanchez here.

Copyright © Angela Scarpa, Anthony Wells and Tony Attwood 2013

The children asked Ms. Baker for help, "Ms. Baker, we feel scared and angry, can you help us?" Since the children had their toys taken away, Ms. Baker suggested that they play a game without using toys. So, they all played Duck, Duck, Goose.

- Insert game picture here.

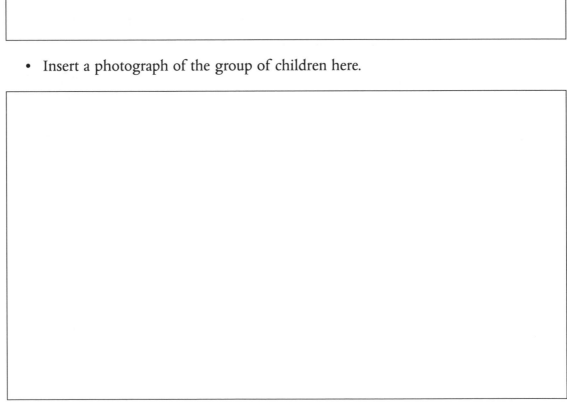

- Insert a photograph of the group of children here.

Copyright © Angela Scarpa, Anthony Wells and Tony Attwood 2013
The STAMP Treatment Manual

After using their tools, Johnny, Billy and Sally felt better and they were having so much fun playing a game together that they did not need their toys. So, the wizard decided to join them and gave them all their toys back for being such smart kids.

- Insert picture of children's location (e.g., a building) here.

The end!

Copyright © Angela Scarpa, Anthony Wells and Tony Attwood 2013

✓

Resource 20

Behavior Monitoring Sheet

Name: _____

Date: _____

Period of observation: From _____ o'clock to _____ o'clock

Instructions: Please use the sheet on the following page to monitor the number of "meltdown" episodes that involved outbursts of anger or anxiety that occurred in the home or while the child was with the family.

Note: A "meltdown" is a child being unable to maintain emotional control and behaving or speaking inappropriately in anger or anxiety. For anxiety, this may also include avoidance of the situation, trembling, freezing, extreme fidgeting, or crying. The meltdown can be any level of intensity or duration.

Use one sheet per day for seven days, starting today. If there are more than 12 episodes in one day, please track and rate others in the space below.

Rate the intensity on a scale from 1 to 10 where 1 = not intense and 10 = extremely intense.

Duration should be measured in the number of minutes (e.g., five minutes).

	1st	2nd	3rd	4th	5th	6th
Time of episode						
Place of episode						
Intensity (1 to 10)						
Duration (in minutes)						
	7th	8th	9th	10th	11th	12th
Time of episode						
Place of episode						
Intensity (1 to 10)						
Duration (in minutes)						

Copyright © Angela Scarpa, Anthony Wells and Tony Attwood 2013
The STAMP Treatment Manual

GROUP REWARD/ CELEBRATION!

This session will focus on review, assessments, and a celebration for completing the group.

1. Cool Down

Time	Schedule/Activity
2 minutes	• Carpet squares/chairs
	• Poster board with schedule and Velcro arrow
	• Poster board with rules
	• Sticker chart

Supplies

Everyone relaxes with a cool down (stretch and breathe) and then sits on a seat/carpet square.

Review the rules for group and remind the children that they can earn stickers if they "follow the rules and use their tools."

2. Welcome

Time	Supplies
8 minutes	• Poster board with photo of each child
	• Poster with words from the Welcome Song
	• Toy microphone (optional)
	• Poster board(s) with list of tools
	• Poster board with four reasons to stay calm

Schedule/Activity

Acknowledge and greet everyone with the Welcome Song (see Session 2).

Remind children of the four reasons we want to stay calm (i.e., to feel better, to think better, to stay out of trouble, and to make and keep friends). Refer to the poster that has the four reasons listed.

Review last week's session (reviewing all our tools by making a commercial).

Review the personalized toolboxes the children did for their home project. What are their favorite tools that help them the most?

3. Singing

Time

5 minutes

Supplies

- Song typed on paper (hint: put one verse per page in large letters and hold up one page at a time for children to follow along)

Schedule/Activity

Say to the children:

💬 Let's practice singing our whole If I'm Angry (or Anxious) and I Know It song!

Sing all the verses together from the beginning, pointing to the words on the board (see Resource 8).

💬 Verse 1: If I'm angry and I know it, *use my tools* (repeat). If I'm angry and I know it, I can use my tools to slow it. If I'm angry and I know it, *use my tools.*

Verse 2: If I'm angry and I know it, *count and breathe* (repeat). If I'm angry and I know it, I can use my tools to slow it. If I'm angry and I know it, *count and breathe.*

Verse 3: If I'm angry and I know it, *stretch and move* (repeat). If I'm angry and I know it, I can use my tools to slow it. If I'm angry and I know it, *stretch and move.*

Verse 4: If I'm angry and I know it, *ask for help* (repeat). If I'm angry and I know it, I can use my tools to slow it. If I'm angry and I know it, *ask for help.*

Verse 5: If I'm angry and I know it, *change my thoughts* (repeat). If I'm angry and I know it, I can use my tools to slow it. If I'm angry and I know it, *change my thoughts.*

Verse 6: If I'm angry and I know it, *do special things* (repeat). If I'm angry and I know it, I can use my tools to slow it. If I'm angry and I know it, *do special things.*

Repeat first verse.

4. Story/Video

Time

5 minutes

Supplies

- Video camera and monitor for viewing

Schedule/Activity

Say to the children:

💬 Let's watch our video commercial. We're all stars!

At the end of session, give each child a copy of the video to keep and watch at home when they want to remember the group. If parental permission was not obtained, be sure to distribute only individual videos.

5. Assessments

Time

15 minutes

Supplies

- Assessment measures

Schedule/Activity

Complete the same self-report assessments (Appendix C) as pre-treatment with each child:

- Child Measure: What Makes You Angry?
- Child Measure: What Makes You Anxious?
- Child Measure: Ben and the Bullies
- Child Measure: James and His Reading Group

6. Snack/Party and Goodbyes

Time

25 minutes

Supplies

- Digital camera
- Special treats/snacks from staff and from home
- Copies of video
- Certificates

Schedule/Activity

Take a group photo of the children.

Parents can join their children for the party.

Show the video again with parents present and distribute videos.

Distribute certificates of completion (Resource 21).

Sincerely congratulate each child and parent and thank them for coming to the group. Remind the children to use their tools and to watch their video or read their group story when they want to remember the things they learned in the group.

Group Reward/Celebration!

This session will focus on review, assessments, and a celebration for completing the group.

1. Cool Down

2. Welcome

3. Singing: If I'm Angry and I Know It or If I'm Anxious and I Know It

4. Story/Video: Our video commercial

5. Assessments (collect the behavior monitoring sheet and complete the remaining same self-report assessments as pre-treatment):

   ○ Parent Questions

   ○ Parent Measure: What Makes My Child Angry?

   ○ Parent Measure: What Makes My Child Anxious?

   ○ Parent Measure: Consumer Satisfaction/Evaluation Survey

6. Snack/Party and Goodbyes

   ○ Take a group photo of the children.

   ○ Parents can join their children for the party.

   ○ Show the video again with parents present and distribute videos.

   ○ Distribute certificates of completion.

Copyright © Angela Scarpa, Anthony Wells and Tony Attwood 2013
The STAMP Treatment Manual

Home Projects

- We hope you enjoyed this group and learned some helpful techniques. *Keep practicing with your child.* They learned new skills here, but they will continue to experience challenges. The skills will only become automatic with practice in their natural environments. When they need a refresher, *watch the review video or read Our Group Story* with your child. This is especially useful to do right before an event or outing where you know the child might need to use their tools. Most of all, model the tools yourself when you are with your child. You are their best teacher!

- *Keep an ongoing success diary* for your child. Make a note when they successfully used a tool to tackle a situation. Write down what strategy they used and give them some praise and a sticker (or any other small reward) to show them how well they have done.

- Appendix A contains a list of the stories we read throughout this group. *Re-read these stories with your child* every so often as additional reminders.

A big "Thank You" to the parents for giving us this wonderful opportunity to work with your children and develop this service! We have enjoyed getting to know you and each of your children.

STAMP GROUP

Congratulations!

You have completed the STAMP K-1 Group
and are awarded this certificate in recognition
of your accomplishments.

_____   _____

Signature   Date

Copyright © Angela Scarpa, Anthony Wells and Tony Attwood 2013
The STAMP Treatment Manual

APPENDIX A
CHILDREN'S STORIES USED IN STAMP

- *Mr. Happy* by Roger Hargreaves

- *If You're Happy and You Know It* by Jane Cabrera

- *A Boy and a Bear* by Lori Lite

- *A Boy and a Turtle* by Lori Lite

- *The Chocolate Covered Cookie Tantrum* by Deborah Blumenthal

- *Knuffle Bunny: A Cautionary Tale* by Mo Willems

- *Otto Goes to the Beach* by Todd Parr

- *Otto Goes to Bed* by Todd Parr

- *Things That Make You Feel Good, Things That Make You Feel Bad* by Todd Parr

- *Reading Makes You Feel Good* by Todd Parr

- *The Social Skills Picture Book* by Jed Baker (particularly the lesson on "Keeping Calm," p. 135)

✓

APPENDIX B
PARENT ASSESSMENTS

Parent Questions

1. On a scale from 1 to 10, please rate how confident *you* feel in managing your child's anger.

1	2	3	4	5	6	7	8	9	10

Not at all
confident

Extremely
confident

2. On a scale from 1 to 10, please rate how confident you perceive *your child* is in managing his/her own anger.

1	2	3	4	5	6	7	8	9	10

Not at all
confident

Extremely
confident

3. On a scale from 1 to 10, please rate how confident *you* feel in managing your child's *anxiety*.

1	2	3	4	5	6	7	8	9	10

Not at all
confident

Extremely
confident

4. On a scale from 1 to 10, please rate how confident you perceive *your child* is in managing his/her own *anxiety*.

1	2	3	4	5	6	7	8	9	10

Not at all
confident

Extremely
confident

Copyright © Angela Scarpa, Anthony Wells and Tony Attwood 2013
The STAMP Treatment Manual

Parent Measure: What Makes My Child Angry?

Follow the instructions below for each point on the following list of statements to identify what makes your child angry.

1. Place a tick next to each item that makes your child angry.

2. For each item ticked, indicate how angry it would make your child feel on a scale of 1 to 10 (with 1 being just a little angry, 5 being moderately angry, and 10 being very angry).

3. For each item ticked, rate how frequently your child has an angry reaction (with 1 being hardly ever, 2 being sometimes, 3 being often, and 4 being very often).

1. When people talk about my child behind his/her back: ☐

   How angry would it make your child (on a scale of 1 to 10)? ☐

   How frequently does your child respond with anger? ☐

2. When my child get his/her work wrong: ☐

   How angry would it make your child (on a scale of 1 to 10)? ☐

   How frequently does your child respond with anger? ☐

3. When other people get hurt: ☐

   How angry would it make your child (on a scale of 1 to 10)? ☐

   How frequently does your child respond with anger? ☐

4. When others won't play with my child: ☐

   How angry would it make your child (on a scale of 1 to 10)? ☐

   How frequently does your child respond with anger? ☐

5. When my child is treated unfairly: ☐

   How angry would it make your child (on a scale of 1 to 10)? ☐

   How frequently does your child respond with anger? ☐

6. When my child is shouted at: ☐

   How angry would it make your child (on a scale of 1 to 10)? ☐

   How frequently does your child respond with anger? ☐

7. When people interfere with his/her games: ☐

   How angry would it make your child (on a scale of 1 to 10)? ☐

   How frequently does your child respond with anger? ☐

Copyright © Angela Scarpa, Anthony Wells and Tony Attwood 2013

8. When people stop my child from doing what he/she wants to do: ☐

How angry would it make your child (on a scale of 1 to 10)? ☐

How frequently does your child respond with anger? ☐

9. When others get more attention than my child does: ☐

How angry would it make your child (on a scale of 1 to 10)? ☐

How frequently does your child respond with anger? ☐

10. When people call my child names: ☐

How angry would it make your child (on a scale of 1 to 10)? ☐

How frequently does your child respond with anger? ☐

11. When they are losing a game: ☐

How angry would it make your child (on a scale of 1 to 10)? ☐

How frequently does your child respond with anger? ☐

12. When people say mean things about his/her family. ☐

How angry would it make your child (on a scale of 1 to 10)? ☐

How frequently does your child respond with anger? ☐

13. When people bully his/her friends: ☐

How angry would it make your child (on a scale of 1 to 10)? ☐

How frequently does your child respond with anger? ☐

14. When someone calls my child a liar: ☐

How angry would it make your child (on a scale of 1 to 10)? ☐

How frequently does your child respond with anger? ☐

15. When someone pushes my child: ☐

How angry would it make your child (on a scale of 1 to 10)? ☐

How frequently does your child respond with anger? ☐

16. When my child gets told off and others do not: ☐

How angry would it make your child (on a scale of 1 to 10)? ☐

How frequently does your child respond with anger? ☐

17. When things get broken: ☐

How angry would it make your child (on a scale of 1 to 10)? ☐

How frequently does your child respond with anger? ☐

Copyright © Angela Scarpa, Anthony Wells and Tony Attwood 2013
The STAMP Treatment Manual

18. When someone takes his/her things: ☐

How angry would it make your child (on a scale of 1 to 10)? ☐

How frequently does your child respond with anger? ☐

19. When there is a lot of noise and my child is trying to concentrate: ☐

How angry would it make your child (on a scale of 1 to 10)? ☐

How frequently does your child respond with anger? ☐

20. When my child has to do something that he/she does not want to do: ☐

How angry would it make your child (on a scale of 1 to 10)? ☐

How frequently does your child respond with anger? ☐

21. When my child is yelled at in front of his/her friends: ☐

How angry would it make your child (on a scale of 1 to 10)? ☐

How frequently does your child respond with anger? ☐

22. When they get interrupted: ☐

How angry would it make your child (on a scale of 1 to 10)? ☐

How frequently does your child respond with anger? ☐

23. When people don't give my child a chance: ☐

How angry would it make your child (on a scale of 1 to 10)? ☐

How frequently does your child respond with anger? ☐

24. When other people are angry: ☐

How angry would it make your child (on a scale of 1 to 10)? ☐

How frequently does your child respond with anger? ☐

25. When people don't listen to him/her: ☐

How angry would it make your child (on a scale of 1 to 10)? ☐

How frequently does your child respond with anger? ☐

26. When people don't understand him/her: ☐

How angry would it make your child (on a scale of 1 to 10)? ☐

How frequently does your child respond with anger? ☐

Copyright © Angela Scarpa, Anthony Wells and Tony Attwood 2013

You can also add some of your own situations that make your child angry that have not been listed:

1. _____

2. _____

3. _____

Parent Measure: What Makes My Child Anxious?

Sometimes we feel anxious, frightened or worried. Follow the instructions below for each point on the following list of statements to identify what makes your child anxious.

1. Place a tick next to each item below if it makes your child feel anxious, frightened, or worried.

2. For each item ticked, indicate how anxious it would make your child feel on a scale of 1 to 10 (with 1 being a just a little anxious, 5 being moderately anxious, and 10 being very anxious).

3. For each item ticked, rate how frequently your child has an anxious reaction (with 1 being hardly ever, 2 being sometimes, 3 being often, and 4 being very often).

1. Being teased at school: ☐

   How angry would it make your child (on a scale of 1 to 10)? ☐

   How frequently does your child respond with anxiety? ☐

2. Getting a new teacher in school: ☐

   How angry would it make your child (on a scale of 1 to 10)? ☐

   How frequently does your child respond with anxiety? ☐

3. Not getting to sleep: ☐

   How angry would it make your child (on a scale of 1 to 10)? ☐

   How frequently does your child respond with anxiety? ☐

4. Someone hurting him/her on purpose at school: ☐

   How angry would it make your child (on a scale of 1 to 10)? ☐

   How frequently does your child respond with anxiety? ☐

Copyright © Angela Scarpa, Anthony Wells and Tony Attwood 2013
The STAMP Treatment Manual

5. Being bitten by a poisonous snake or spider: ☐

    How angry would it make your child (on a scale of 1 to 10)? ☐

    How frequently does your child respond with anxiety? ☐

6. Making a mistake on his/her school work: ☐

    How angry would it make your child (on a scale of 1 to 10)? ☐

    How frequently does your child respond with anxiety? ☐

7. Losing his/her temper: ☐

    How angry would it make your child (on a scale of 1 to 10)? ☐

    How frequently does your child respond with anxiety? ☐

8. Vomiting: ☐

    How angry would it make your child (on a scale of 1 to 10)? ☐

    How frequently does your child respond with anxiety? ☐

9. Hearing certain noises like _____ : ☐

    How angry would it make your child (on a scale of 1 to 10)? ☐

    How frequently does your child respond with anxiety? ☐

10. The taste or feel of foods such as _____ : ☐

    How angry would it make your child (on a scale of 1 to 10)? ☐

    How frequently does your child respond with anxiety? ☐

11. His/her dreams: ☐

    How angry would it make your child (on a scale of 1 to 10)? ☐

    How frequently does your child respond with anxiety? ☐

12. Being alone: ☐

    How angry would it make your child (on a scale of 1 to 10)? ☐

    How frequently does your child respond with anxiety? ☐

13. Crying: ☐

    How angry would it make your child (on a scale of 1 to 10)? ☐

    How frequently does your child respond with anxiety? ☐

14. Being yelled at by a teacher: ☐

    How angry would it make your child (on a scale of 1 to 10)? ☐

    How frequently does your child respond with anxiety? ☐

Copyright © Angela Scarpa, Anthony Wells and Tony Attwood 2013

15. Having to make choices about things:

How angry would it make your child (on a scale of 1 to 10)?

How frequently does your child respond with anxiety?

16. What other kids think of him/her:

How angry would it make your child (on a scale of 1 to 10)?

How frequently does your child respond with anxiety?

17. Doing his/her homework:

How angry would it make your child (on a scale of 1 to 10)?

How frequently does your child respond with anxiety?

18. Going to school:

How angry would it make your child (on a scale of 1 to 10)?

How frequently does your child respond with anxiety?

19. The playground:

How angry would it make your child (on a scale of 1 to 10)?

How frequently does your child respond with anxiety?

20. Having no friends:

How angry would it make your child (on a scale of 1 to 10)?

How frequently does your child respond with anxiety?

21. Looking funny in front of people:

How angry would it make your child (on a scale of 1 to 10)?

How frequently does your child respond with anxiety?

22. Ghosts:

How angry would it make your child (on a scale of 1 to 10)?

How frequently does your child respond with anxiety?

23. Going to the hospital:

How angry would it make your child (on a scale of 1 to 10)?

How frequently does your child respond with anxiety?

24. Being sent to the principal's office:

How angry would it make your child (on a scale of 1 to 10)?

How frequently does your child respond with anxiety?

Copyright © Angela Scarpa, Anthony Wells and Tony Attwood 2013
The STAMP Treatment Manual

25. High places: ☐

How angry would it make your child (on a scale of 1 to 10)? ☐

How frequently does your child respond with anxiety? ☐

26. Being around lots of people: ☐

How angry would it make your child (on a scale of 1 to 10)? ☐

How frequently does your child respond with anxiety? ☐

27. Thunderstorms: ☐

How angry would it make your child (on a scale of 1 to 10)? ☐

How frequently does your child respond with anxiety? ☐

28. Parents fighting: ☐

How angry would it make your child (on a scale of 1 to 10)? ☐

How frequently does your child respond with anxiety? ☐

29. Germs: ☐

How angry would it make your child (on a scale of 1 to 10)? ☐

How frequently does your child respond with anxiety? ☐

30. Not being able to breathe: ☐

How angry would it make your child (on a scale of 1 to 10)? ☐

How frequently does your child respond with anxiety? ☐

31. A test at school: ☐

How angry would it make your child (on a scale of 1 to 10)? ☐

How frequently does your child respond with anxiety? ☐

You can also add some of your own situations that make your child anxious (frightened, scared, or worried) that have not been listed.

1. _____

2. _____

3. _____

Copyright © Angela Scarpa, Anthony Wells and Tony Attwood 2013

Parent Measure: Behavior Monitoring Sheet

Name: _____

Date: _____

Period of observation: From _____ o'clock to _____ o'clock

Instructions: Please use the sheet on the following page to monitor the number of "meltdown" episodes that involved outbursts of anger or anxiety that occurred in the home or while the child was with the family.

Note: A "meltdown" is a child being unable to maintain emotional control and behaving or speaking inappropriately in anger or anxiety. For anxiety, this may also include avoidance of the situation, trembling, freezing, extreme fidgeting, or crying. The meltdown can be any level of intensity or duration.

Use one sheet per day for seven days, starting today. If there are more than 12 episodes in one day, please track and rate others in the space below.

Rate the intensity on a scale from 1 to 10 where 1 = not intense and 10 = extremely intense.

Duration should be measured in the number of minutes (e.g., five minutes).

	1st	2nd	3rd	4th	5th	6th
Time of episode						
Place of episode						
Intensity (1 to 10)						
Duration (in minutes)						
	7th	8th	9th	10th	11th	12th
Time of episode						
Place of episode						
Intensity (1 to 10)						
Duration (in minutes)						

Copyright © Angela Scarpa, Anthony Wells and Tony Attwood 2013
The STAMP Treatment Manual

Parent Measure: Consumer Satisfaction/Evaluation Survey

1. What is your level of satisfaction with the Stress and Anger Management Program (tick one)?

   ☐ Very Satisfied

   ☐ Somewhat Satisfied

   ☐ Satisfied

   ☐ Slightly Satisfied

   ☐ Not Satisfied

2. Please explain your answer to the question above.

   _____

   _____

3. What did you see as the strengths of this program? What went well?

   _____

   _____

4. What did you see as the weaknesses of this program? What could be improved?

   _____

   _____

5. What changes, if any, did you notice in you and your child after being in this program?

   _____

   _____

Copyright © Angela Scarpa, Anthony Wells and Tony Attwood 2013

APPENDIX C
CHILD ASSESSMENTS

Child Measure: What Makes You Angry?

Say to the child: "Here is a list of things that makes some kids angry. Which ones make you angry?"

Show them the following 1 to 3 scale:

1: Little angry   2: Medium angry   3: Very angry

For each point below, ask "Does this make you angry?"

If they answer yes, then ask: "How angry does it make you feel: a little angry, medium angry, or very angry?"

1. When people talk about you without you knowing: ☐ Yes ☐ No, Rating: ____

2. When you get your work wrong: ☐ Yes ☐ No, Rating: ____

3. When other people get hurt: ☐ Yes ☐ No, Rating: ____

4. When others won't play with you: ☐ Yes ☐ No, Rating: ____

5. When you are treated unfairly: ☐ Yes ☐ No, Rating: ____

6. When you are shouted at: ☐ Yes ☐ No, Rating: ____

7. When people mess up your games: ☐ Yes ☐ No, Rating: ____

8. When people stop you from doing what you want to do: ☐ Yes ☐ No, Rating: ____

9. When others get more attention than you: ☐ Yes ☐ No, Rating: ____

10. When people call you names: ☐ Yes ☐ No, Rating: ____

11. When you are losing a game: ☐ Yes ☐ No, Rating: ____

12. When people say mean things about your family: ☐ Yes ☐ No, Rating: ____

Copyright © Angela Scarpa, Anthony Wells and Tony Attwood 2013
The STAMP Treatment Manual

13. When people bully your friends: ☐ Yes ☐ No, Rating: _____

14. When someone calls you a liar: ☐ Yes ☐ No, Rating: _____

15. When someone pushes you: ☐ Yes ☐ No, Rating: _____

16. When you get in trouble and others don't: ☐ Yes ☐ No, Rating: _____

17. When things get broken: ☐ Yes ☐ No, Rating: _____

18. When someone takes your things: ☐ Yes ☐ No, Rating: _____

19. When there is a lot of noise and you are trying to concentrate: ☐ Yes ☐ No, Rating: _____

20. When you have to do something you don't want to do: ☐ Yes ☐ No, Rating: _____

21. When you are yelled at in front of your friends: ☐ Yes ☐ No, Rating: _____

22. When you get interrupted: ☐ Yes ☐ No, Rating: _____

23. When people don't give you a chance: ☐ Yes ☐ No, Rating: _____

24. When other people are angry: ☐ Yes ☐ No, Rating: _____

25. When people don't listen to you: ☐ Yes ☐ No, Rating: _____

26. When people don't understand you: ☐ Yes ☐ No, Rating: _____

Ask the child: "Are there other things that make you angry?"

1. _____

2. _____

3. _____

Child Measure: What Makes You Anxious?

Say to the child: "Sometimes children feel anxious. This means they can feel scared or nervous or worried. Here is a list of things that make some kids feel scared, nervous, or worried. Which ones make you feel this way?"

Show them the following 1 to 3 scale:

1: Little anxious   2: Medium anxious   3: Very anxious

For each point below, ask "Does this make you anxious (or scared, nervous, or worried)?"

Copyright © Angela Scarpa, Anthony Wells and Tony Attwood 2013
The STAMP Treatment Manual

If they answer yes, then ask: "How anxious (or scared, nervous, or worried) does it make you feel when you think about it: a little anxious, medium anxious, or very anxious?"

1. Being teased at school: ☐ Yes ☐ No, Rating: _____
2. Getting a new teacher in school: ☐ Yes ☐ No, Rating: _____
3. Not getting to sleep: ☐ Yes ☐ No, Rating: _____
4. Someone hurting you on purpose at school: ☐ Yes ☐ No, Rating: _____
5. Being bitten by a poisonous snake or spider: ☐ Yes ☐ No, Rating: _____
6. Making a mistake on your school work: ☐ Yes ☐ No, Rating: _____
7. Losing your temper: ☐ Yes ☐ No, Rating: _____
8. Vomiting: ☐ Yes ☐ No, Rating: _____
9. Hearing certain noises: ☐ Yes ☐ No, Rating: _____
10. The taste or feel of certain foods: ☐ Yes ☐ No, Rating: _____
11. Your dreams: ☐ Yes ☐ No, Rating: _____
12. Being alone: ☐ Yes ☐ No, Rating: _____
13. Crying: ☐ Yes ☐ No, Rating: _____
14. Being yelled at by a teacher: ☐ Yes ☐ No, Rating: _____
15. Having to make choices about things: ☐ Yes ☐ No, Rating: _____
16. What other kids think of you: ☐ Yes ☐ No, Rating: _____
17. Doing your homework: ☐ Yes ☐ No, Rating: _____
18. Going to school: ☐ Yes ☐ No, Rating: _____
19. The playground: ☐ Yes ☐ No, Rating: _____
20. Having no friends: ☐ Yes ☐ No, Rating: _____
21. Looking funny in front of people: ☐ Yes ☐ No, Rating: _____
22. Ghosts: ☐ Yes ☐ No, Rating: _____
23. Going to the hospital: ☐ Yes ☐ No, Rating: _____
24. Being sent to the principal's office: ☐ Yes ☐ No, Rating: _____
25. High places: ☐ Yes ☐ No, Rating: _____
26. Being around lots of people: ☐ Yes ☐ No, Rating: _____
27. Thunderstorms: ☐ Yes ☐ No, Rating: _____
28. Parents fighting: ☐ Yes ☐ No, Rating: _____
29. Germs: ☐ Yes ☐ No, Rating: _____

Copyright © Angela Scarpa, Anthony Wells and Tony Attwood 2013
The STAMP Treatment Manual

✓

30. Not being able to breathe: ☐ Yes ☐ No, Rating: _____

31. A test at school: ☐ Yes ☐ No, Rating: _____

Ask the child: "Are there other things that make you anxious (or scared, nervous, or worried)?"

1. _____

2. _____

3. _____

Child Measure: Ben and the Bullies

Ben is in Mrs. Smith's class. Ben has many friends in his class and he often plays with them during recess.

There are three boys in his grade who always bother him during recess. They like to find people to tease and get people in trouble. They are not Ben's friends. Sometimes they can be really mean and they hit Ben and call him names. Ben gets mad when they bother him and he hits them back.

It is recess now, and Ben is playing with his friends. He brought his favorite toy from his house—a robot. The three boys, who always bother him, come over and grab his robot. They will not give him back his favorite toy. If he hits them he won't be able to play at recess.

- What could Ben do so that he stays calm and does not get mad with them?

Copyright © Angela Scarpa, Anthony Wells and Tony Attwood 2013

Child Measure: James and His Reading Group

James's teacher is Mrs. Smith. She is a nice teacher. He really likes being in her class. She keeps the kids quiet and doesn't allow them to make fun of each other. James has trouble reading out loud and she helps him when he messes up or doesn't know a word.

On Tuesday, James has reading group and he has to read in front of the whole group. He is scared that he won't do well and the other children will make fun of him. When Tuesday comes, James goes to school and finds that his teacher, Mrs. Smith, is sick and will not be in class that day but he is still going to have to read in front of his group. James gets very nervous because he thinks the other kids will make noise and Mrs. Smith is not there to help. James is worried that he might mess up and the kids will make fun of him.

- What can James do so that he doesn't feel so scared?

Copyright © Angela Scarpa, Anthony Wells and Tony Attwood 2013
The STAMP Treatment Manual